TOM CUNNINGHAM, BRAD SZOLLOSE AND JOHN WESTLEY CLAYTON PRESENT...

VOLUME 8

JOURNEYS TO SUCCESS

SALES PROFESSIONALS EDITION

9 INTERNATIONAL AUTHORS SHARE THEIR **MOST POWERFUL SALES STORIES IN THE TOUGHEST BUSINESS SECTORS. BASED** ON **THE SUCCESS PRINCIPLES OF NAPOLEON HILL**

JOURNEYS
TO
SUCCESS

VOLUME 8

SALES PROFESSIONALS EDITION

Publisher: John Westley Clayton

www.johnwestley.com

info@johnwestley.com

ISBN 978-1-947560-04-8

Cover Photo Credit:

ShutterStock ID: 130099706

By ASDF_MEDIA

Business people shaking hands, finishing up a meeting

Table of Contents

Dedication

This book is dedicated to those who take the risk of giving up a "*safe*" 9 to 5 job to create a career in the greatest profession in the world, as a salesperson.

Changing lives, one sale at a time.

Acknowledgements

We would like to thank Tom "*too tall*" Cunningham for creating the Journeys To Success brand. Without Tom, this book series would have never happened.

We pay tribute to Tom.

We started this projesct with Tom and he passed away April 9th ,2018.

Foreword

Sales. The mere mention of the word can drive some into a cold sweat, others to run away, while a small percentage of us lean in and get busy. I love sales. Always have. But I have never sold a thing. I know what you're thinking... "*But Joe, you are in the Guinness Book of World Records for selling 13,001 new cars and trucks at retail price during a fifteen-year selling career.*"

Yes. That's the result.

In a profession where an average salesperson sells 6 to 7 cars a month, I was selling 7 cars a day. Yet, I never really sold a single car...instead, I sold me.

"What do you mean by that Joe?"

People buy from you because of something that makes you unique. They sense it. It's deep down inside, on a subconscious level, where they sense that you are a trusted friend.

Once people buy from Joe Girard, they know, there is no one else like me. That is what caused those 13,001 cars to sell; it was ME, and ME alone.

My key to success was to send out personalized greeting cards to customers and prospective customers. I didn't do this as some sort of gimmick. I did it because I genuinely like people. It was important for me to stay in touch with this "*virtual family.*" I cared about their well-being and they seemed to respond in kind.

Customers always do business with people they suspect they could be friends with.

ATNA: All Talk And No Action

I am honored to be a part of this Sales Edition in The Journeys to Success series. When I heard that Tom "*too tall*" Cunningham had passed away, I was shocked. As a guest on his radio show, Tom had the unique ability to draw out the very best from his guests. He made me feel at home. I am more than honored to have known him...and saddened that the world has lost a best friend.

Get ready. Rarely do successful people reveal their secrets...until now. The stories you are about to read are by real people on the front lines who figured out their own unique methods for selling. I suggest you take copious notes, dog-ear your favorite pages and underline the deepest passages.

Napoleon Hill wrote in-depth about discovering your own burning desire. What drives you to do what you do? I call that "*the spark*." And sparks create a fire. I hope you discover within these pages the powerful spark that leads you to the ultimate success in your life.

I like you. Be good to others. You can do this.

God bless.

Now go get em.

Joe Girard

Introduction

Welcome to another powerful edition of Journeys to Success. I am excited, elated and sad at the same time. Why you may ask? Well, for the past three years, me, Tom Cunningham and John Westley Clayton have handpicked each author in the nine JTS books we've published so far.

That's over 200 authors to date.

Each gets a chance to tell their story of struggle, failure and eventual success. As a publishing team, we get a front row seat to some pretty amazing people. What is an even greater privilege is convincing these people that their personal story matters. Despite their successes the common thread is that of humility and appreciation for the path they have chosen.

The cornerstone of all Napoleon Hill works, is that you work with the principles in your real life. Which isn't always easy. Many of you know first hand what it's like to try and keep a positive mental attitude despite your current circumstances.

With that being said, it is with sad news that I announce the passing of our little brother, friend, speaker, colleague and business partner, Tom Cunningham. Many of you know that Tom suffered with Rheumatoid Arthritis for over 50 years starting at the age of 5.

Imagine being in constant pain for that long and you will begin to understand Tom. With four hip replacements, two shoulders and four knee replacements and one ankle fusion through the years, made Tom sound more and more like the intro to the Six Million Dollar Man television show… "*We can rebuild him. We have the technology. We will make him better than he was.*"

The fact that he could answer "*amazing*" every time someone asked him how he was doing, is beyond my sense of understanding. He was a true warrior who had the ability to transcend his physical body.

In the last months of his life I could hear exhaustion in his voice. As his cohost on the Journeys To Success Radio Network, Tom and I would banter back and forth with his guests. But in February of 2018, and three guest authors in a row, I could hear Tom was in severe pain…more so than ever before.

As I signed on for our second interview, he greeted me with a gruff noise. A sound caught between stubbing your toe, and a crotchety old man who was tired of life. It wasn't a word at all. It was just a sound. Then silence. I asked "*where's the 'amazing!' part.*" His response was eerily a foreboding of things to come… "That is my 'amazing' nowadays."

Tom was fighting an infection in his knee for months that had caused swelling and inflammation throughout his entire body. Bone pain is different. It throbs at the core, and can feel endless…and in a show of true strength, Tom refused the opioid meds that could have eased the pain, but put his mental state out of commission.

On April 6th, 2018, Tom went into the hospital to have his knee replacement scraped, adjusted, or removed. The latter was not an option for him because it meant he couldn't go anywhere for 6 months.

Walking, bathing, going to the bathroom...everything, would have required assistance.

With his loving wife Kim by his side, he admitted being truly scared for the very first time in his life. Perhaps he knew this would be his last. The surgery went well, and Tom appeared to be recovering on Sunday morning. He was posting on Facebook, sending us messages, and seemed in good spirits

But alas, he barely made it to Monday morning, dying ten minutes after midnight.

Through the grace of God, I know that Tom is in a better place...a place free of pain.

We are saddened here at Journeys to Success by the passing of our founder Tom "too tall" Cunningham. Taylor Tagg will be carrying on the radio show and scheduling interviews while John Westley Clayton and I will continue the book series.

Tom's legacy will live on through all who knew him, and the authors he has brought to each and every project.

My favorite thing to do was to make Tom laugh. His laugh was contagious, and the more I teased him, the more he laughed with childlike enthusiasm. That enthusiasm for life and new adventures was his superpower. His love for humanity and every guest to grace his show was treated with compassion and curiosity.

Tom never really understood that people would fly halfway around the world to see him speak. He was special and never knew it. His wife Kim knew it. Those of us who worked with him, knew it. The people who heard him speak for the first time knew it. It was so easy to become a fan.

From here on out, if you ask me how I'm doing, my response will be "simply, amazing."

We miss you my friend.

Brad Szollose

CHAPTER 1

Sales= Motive + Communication

By Alex Alfaro

We are all salesmen. I have always heard statements such as, "*I don't like sales, sales are not for me, I can never do sales, I don't have the outgoing personality for sales*". Well, sorry to break it to you but you are in sales and you can get much better at it than you think.

Merriam-Webster has the definition of Sales as, "*the operations and activities involved in promoting and selling goods or services, or the amount of goods or services sold in any given time period*". I am going to focus on the "*promoting and selling*" portion of this definition, although I don't necessarily agree that its limited to only goods and services. If you ask someone the question, "*What is a salesman?*", you will get a multitude of different answers or opinions. Everyone has their vision of a salesman based on personal experiences. These experiences have shaped their beliefs and opinions, but more than likely, the picture that comes to mind is someone trying to get you to buy some sort of goods or service; as stated by the Webster definition. The car salesman that walks over to you as soon as you park your car on the lot, pushing the next hottest car, or those pesky people that follow you around the store, telling you about the current sale and hover around you even after you tell them that you are just looking. Sales is much more than that. It is not a profession and it is not limited to goods & services. Sales is a daily part of everyone's life. Sales is an understanding of the person's motive, and it is a form of effective communication. Although the remaining chapters of this book will consist of sales stories in the toughest business sectors based on the success principles of Napoleon Hill, I wanted to start this first chapter with something different. Sales from a new perspective, one that helps you understand that we are all in sales and we are all always selling. Then, I would like to provide you with some tools that you can use immediately to help communicate better and sell effectively. I would also ask that while reading the remaining chapters, you begin to practice these tools by looking out for the 9 basic motives and figure out the representational system of each one of the authors. I will discuss in detail what that means later in this chapter.

My name is Alex Alfaro. I am the CEO and Founder of SCL Group, a Logistics Consulting Firm. We work with companies looking to create efficiency, optimize vendor relationships, and ultimately save money on freight. SCL Group has done business with companies of all sizes, from the small startup company trying to figure out how to get their product from point A to point B, to the large multinational corporations such as Adidas, Vans, Converse, Fox Media Company, and most recently, the NBA. I have never considered myself a salesman, yet I have walked into some of the largest companies and have been able to distinguish a motive and communicate value effectively. In 1999, I read *Think and Grow Rich* by Napoleon Hill for the first time. I consider this book the foundation and the catalyst to any success that I have had and will continue to have in the future. I am a student of Napoleon Hill's Laws of Success philosophy and in 2015, I became a Certified Instructor for the Napoleon Hill Foundation. I have also studied Neuro-Linguistics Programming (NLP) from one of the founders, Richard Bandler; and became a Master Practitioner. I am no master salesman, I am no sales guru, I don't have a philosophy that you can follow that will multiply your income in 90 days. I have failed, failed often and will continue to fail. Yet, I am excited by that very fact. I am a student of self-development and self-mastery, and I do understand that without failure, neither are possible. I have learned a thing or two on my personal journey to success, and I am grateful, blessed, and excited about this opportunity to share it.

10 Basic Motives

All individual achievements are a result of a motive or a combination of motives. Learn what motivates you and then you can have, be, or do anything you want in life.

When you were a kid and wanted that new toy, you were selling to your parents. When you decided to start caring about what you looked like on the first day of school and put thought into what you would wear, you were selling to the rest of the kids at school. When you went on that first date or courted someone you liked, you were selling. I don't care what the profession is; you are always selling. Whether it be a teacher in the classroom, a fitness trainer, a human resource manager, or a mortgage underwriter, they are all salesmen. Even the parent trying to get the kids to do their homework, brush their teeth, or take out the trash, they are practicing the act of selling. We are selling daily, it's a part of life. Any time you are communicating, you are selling.

First, we must understand that we have no right to ask anybody to do anything at any time without giving them an adequate motive. All salesmanship is the ability to plant an adequate motive in the mind of the prospective buyer. According to Napoleon Hill, there are ten basic motives that inspire all voluntary action. These ten motives constitute success in dealing with other people, for all sane people are engaged in voluntary action because of a motive. Unless you are familiar with the motives that affect success, you can never fully understand other people, and what makes them function.

1. ***Desire for Self-Preservation***- Everyone is motivated in this direction. It's our survival instinct. It is already quite generally understood, but we will point out, however, that in primitive times this motive was useful in defending ones-self against aggressive physical foes. Now it is largely related to the desire for material wealth and the struggle for preservation from want and fear. It is manifested in our society as the desire for economic security.
2. ***The emotion of Love***- The greatest of all motives is love. Love is a psychic force related to our spiritual side. When we speak of love, we refer not merely to physical attraction. We mean love in its bigger, broader sense. Love is the greatest and most powerful motive known.
3. ***The emotion of Fear***- There are 7 basic fears. Some combination of which every person suffers at one time or another. They

can rob you of your personal Initiative and keep you in poverty all your life. All the basic fears must be conquered if you are going to eliminate their negative influence.

1. Fear of poverty
2. Fear of ill health
3. Fear of criticism
4. Fear of the loss of love
5. Fear of old age
6. Fear of the loss of liberty
7. Fear of death

4. ***The emotion of Sex***- Sex is the physical complement of love. Nature carefully applies the principle of a Definite Major Purpose to this motive. The desire for physical expression of the mating instinct is the most powerful of emotions. To satisfy this urge, we develop imagination, fortitude and creative ability that may be totally lacking at other times. if it does not find a useful outlet, it will eventually break through the restraining wall and cause destruction.
5. ***The desire for Life after Death***- This is a very strong motive and it is the one upon which nearly all religious activity is based. A desire for perpetual life is closely allied with the desire for self-preservation and is instinctive.
6. ***The desire for Freedom of Body and Mind***- The basic wish in everyone's heart is the desire to be free and unfettered.
7. ***The desire for Revenge***- Revenge is a motive for action and very strong one. It is a waste of energy and personal power

when you harbor revenge in your mind and heart.

8. ***The emotion of Hate***- Revenge and Hate can be lumped together because although the feeling of getting even with someone seems natural, it is utterly wasteful. It builds or improves nothing or no one. Holding a grudge results in a negative mental attitude, which is the antithesis of the constructive Positive Mental Attitude that is required for success.
9. ***The desire for Self-Expression and Recognition***- You should be working harder for the opportunity to express yourself and to gain public recognition than for any amount of money.
10. ***The desire for Material Gain***- Desire for material gain is fundamental in human nature. If you combine the emotion of love, the emotion of sex and the desire for material wealth, you will have the three emotions that seem to drive the world.

If you think back to any good or bad decision you have made in your life, I can pretty much guarantee you can pinpoint which motive drove that decision. Now, as a salesman if you can first pinpoint what motivates the person you are trying to sell to, you can communicate in a way that triggers that motive. Sales for me equals Motive plus Communication.

When you start to see that telling your child to brush his teeth, getting an employee to do his work, or getting your significant other to jump on that to do list is selling, then you can begin to think about what adequate motive is needed to get them to do what you want them to do. You are in sales, you just didn't know you where.

Representational Systems

All distinctions human beings are able to make concerning our environment and our behavior can be usefully represented through visual, auditory, kinesthetic, olfactory, and gustatory senses.

Now that we have figured out the motive that drives the behavior, the important stage begins; learning how to effectively communicate. In NLP-Neuro Linguistics Programming, there are what are called Presuppositions. A presupposition is a thing tactically assumed beforehand at the beginning of a line of argument or course of action. One of the presuppositions of NLP is that **the meaning of the communication is the response you get**. In other words, if you say something to someone and they respond in a way that you didn't expect, then you failed in the communication. With this in mind, you come to realize that the old adage that communication is a two-way street is actually incorrect; it's a one-way street. You are 100% in control and can make the necessary adjustments if needed to get the response you want or expect.

Human beings experience themselves and the world they live in through the primary modalities of the 5 senses: seeing, hearing, feeling, smelling, and tasting. The sensory modalities by which people encode, organize, store, and attach meaning to perceptual input are referred to as **Representational Systems**. As sensory input is internally processed (re-represented), it is translated into corresponding sensory representations (or maps) that constitute a likeness or synthesis of the original perceptual input. This may seem obvious, yet very important to remember; "*reality*" and our perception of "reality" are not the same. Human beings naturally blend a mix of the different representational systems, yet we all tend to prefer one modality over the other. In order to enhance your own communication skills, we must listen and learn which modality is favored by the person we are communicating with. A simple way to do this is by listening to the types of words and phrases people use and then ask yourself whether these are Visual, Auditory, Kinesthetic, or Olfactory/Gustatory. Once you learn the person's Representational System, you then have information you can utilize effectively in your communication. You can use their words and phrases. You can speak their language, so to speak. In other words, just because you speak the same language, it does not mean you are effectively communicating; you need to speak their dialect. Here are a few samples:

A husband buys his wife flowers, holds his wife's hand on long walks, and does all the little things she wants them to do together. His wife's main representational system is Auditory. If she doesn't hear the words, "I love you" on a regular basis, she will not ever truly feel that her husband loves her. Her husband may be a kinesthetic and represent his love by holding her hand, hugging and touching regularly but by no fault of his, they end up with a complete miscommunication of one another's love and end up in divorce.

A teacher is a visual. When teaching class, she uses her own representational system to teach and uses many pictures and visual aids. All the visual learners get excellent grades because she is speaking the Visual dialect. Auditory and Kinesthetic learners have a hard time learning the material because the Auditory learners don't get to learn through listening and speaking, and the Kinesthetic learners doesn't get to learn through carrying out physical activities. The great teachers learn to utilize all the representational systems when preparing a lesson.

The following are a list of the Representational Systems and the sample words that represent each one. I have listed Olfactory (the sense of smell) and Gustatory (the sense of taste) but most people are dominant in either Visual, Auditory, or Kinesthetic.

Visual (Look/See)

Appear Focus Notice
Perceive Sight

Clarity Glance Observe
Picture Show

Foresee Look Obvious See
Watch

Auditory (Say/Sound/Hear)

Articulate Gossip Interview Noise
Say

Boisterous Hear Listen Remark
Sound

Discuss Inquire Mention
Ring Tell

Kinesthetic (Feel/Do)

Affected Emotional Hassle Pressure Tension

Charge Foundation Hold Shift Touch

Concrete Grasp Motion Solid Unsettled

Olfactory/Gustatory (Smell/Taste)

Aroma Reeks Smells Tasty Spicy

Dank Rotten Sweet Delicious Zesty

Musty Stinks Tangy Bland Bitter

When selling to a visual, you need to paint a picture for them of what you have to offer.

When selling to an auditory, you need to tell them what you can do for them and have more conversation.

When selling to a kinesthetic, you need to get them involved, provide handouts, and use examples that trigger certain feelings and emotions.

Representational System predicates are the process words (verbs, adverbs, adjectives) which people use in their communication to represent their experience internally, either visually, auditory, or kinesthetically. Below are listed some of the more commonly used rep system predicates (phrases) in the business environment.

Visual (See)

An eyeful Appears to me
Beyond a shadow of a doubt

Bird's eye view Catch a glimpse of Clear
cut

Dim view Eye to eye Flashed on

Hazy idea Get a scope on Get a
perspective on

In light of In person Horse
different color

In view of Looks like Make a
scene

Mental image Mental picture
Mind's eye

Naked eye Paint a picture
Photographic memory

Plainly see Pretty as a picture See to it

Short sighted Showing off Sight
for sore eyes

Staring off in space Take a peek
Tunnel Vision

Under your nose Up front Well
defined

Auditory (Hear)

After thought Blabber mouth Clear as a bell

Clearly expressed Call on Describe in detail

Earful Express yourself Give an account of

Give me your ear Grant an audience Heard voices

Hold your tongue Idle talk Inquire into

Keynote speaker Loud and clear Manner of speaking

Pay attention to Power of speech Purrs like a kitten

Outspoken Rap session Rings a bell

State your purpose Tattle tale To tell the truth

Tongue tied Tuned in/turned out Unheard of

Utterly Voiced an opinionWell informed

Word for word Within hearing range

Kinesthetic (Feel)

Sales= Motive + Communication

All washed up Boils down to Chip of the old block

Come to grips with Control Yourself Cool/calm/collected

Firm foundation Floating on thin air Get a handle on

Get a load of this Get in touch with Get the drift of

Get your goat Hand in hand Hang in there!

Hot head Keep your shirt on! Know how

Lay cards on table Light headed Moment of panic

Not following you Pull some strings Sharp as a tack

Slipped my mind Smooth Operator So-So

Start from scratch Stiff upper lip Stuffed shirt

Underhanded Topsy Turvy Too much of a hassle

The value of learning the representational system of the person you are trying to communicate with or "*sell*" should now be crystal clear. The objective in matching Representational System predicates is to match the language in which the listener speaks, thus creating an atmosphere of rapport and understanding. When you speak the same dialect (Visual, Auditory,

Kinesthetic) you can create instant rapport and break down subconscious barriers. We all know that without rapport, it is nearly impossible to get someone to do what you want them to do or buy what you are selling.

At this point, it should be beyond a shadow of a doubt, it should be ringing loud and clear, and we should have a handle on the fact that we are all salesmen. If you can give someone an adequate motive and communicate value in an effective way, then you are on the path to become a master salesman. Sales = Motive plus Communication. Start Now. Learn what motivates you and figure out what your dominant representational system is. Then move on to your immediate family and friends. These tools have helped me navigate and effectively communicate in my personal life as well as in business. If utilized, I know for a fact that it can work wonders for you as well. With constant practice and the use of both ears when listening, you can effectively communicate with others, but more importantly, you can learn to effectively communicate with yourself.

Alex Alfaro | Bio

Alex Alfaro is the CEO and Founder of SCL Group, a Logistics Consulting Firm. He is the managing partner of StuDoc, a student loan consolidation call center. Partner of Priority Debt Relief, which helps people eliminate debt. Founder and CEO of Mental Acuity Group which works with athletes at all levels to achieve peak performance through Mindfulness, Sensory Awareness, Emotional Intelligence, Visualization and Self-Hypnosis.

He is a Certified Instructor for the Napoleon Hill Foundation, and Master Practitioner of NLP- Neuro Linguistic Programming. Throughout his study in the Napoleon Hill's Success Philosophy he was able to turn adversity and failure into success and all his companies are now multimillion-dollar revenue firms. Inspired by Napoleon Hill's "*Think and Grow Rich*" and his 17 Laws of Success he formed Stoic Mastermind Group, a mastermind alliance focused on PMA (Positive Mental Attitude), the 17 Laws of Success, NLP-Neuro Linguistic Programming as taught by the founder Richard Bandler, and Stoicism an ancient Stoic Philosophy that pursues self-mastery, perseverance, and contains some of the greatest wisdom in the history of the world.

CHAPTER 2

Staying Focused on The Winding Road

By Geoffrey A. Brown

Enjoy the ride!

I was ten years deep into my career in sales before I admitted to myself that sales was, indeed, what I wanted to do. Changing jobs in a sales career is not unusual as I'm sure many readers can attest; but answering the continual questions of why you are moving to a new company or entirely new field gets old quickly and often made me feel as though something was wrong with me. Why couldn't I stay with a company or in a particular field?

I spent more hours than I like to admit discussing job changes with my wife. It's not easy starting out in sales, especially the 100% commission positions I gravitated toward. Those positions always seem so promising with high-income opportunities for a hard worker, but there always seemed to be a catch.

I learned more about face-to-face interactions with people selling Honda automobiles in upstate NY than I have probably learned in the past 20 years since I left the position.

It was mid January and I was functionally unemployed. My wife and I were married less than a year and I was biding my time waiting for the Army to send us to Alabama for flight school. Ginger was getting worried because I was unhappy. Not with our newlywed marriage, but with waiting. I didn't know what to do and no one wanted to hire me because I would have to leave them as soon as the US Army called me. We stayed two extra weeks at my inlaws over Christmas. They too were getting worried about us and I kept thinking of that old Ben Franklin saying, "*house guests and fish both start to smell after three days*".

As two weeks became three, we made the decision to head back home to Western NY and our tiny brownstone apartment that we could barely afford. Thank God I had my National Guard weekends to earn a monthly income. Ginger called a couple of employers, set up interviews and told me I was going to go and I was NOT going to tell them that I was leaving when the Army called. That was a real hang up for me back then. It felt very wrong to me to mislead people or lie by omission just to get work, but I had a wife and an apartment and ultimately she was right to force that issue. We have a responsibility to to take care of our families. Getting a job is hard when telling the naked truth about your level of experience or whether or not you plan to stay in that position for years to come. So you omit or sometimes do whatever it takes to feed your family. So that's exactly what I did.

The interview went fantastic and I was hired on the spot. I remember the sales manager saying, "Mr. Brown, you are exactly the kind of go-getter I want on my team. When can you start?"

Perhaps I am jaded now, or I was extra naive back then, but I really believed him when he made me feel special. I believed that he really was excited to have me selling his cars. A "*go-getter*" ... yep, that was me. Within a year, however, I realized they would hire anyone, and I mean anyone. I started selling Hondas at the city dealership, and the sales manager's name was Tony. Tony was a stereotypical kind of a guy who was from New York City, but was now living upstate. He spent more money on his suits than some of the used cars on our lot were worth, and when he wasn't buying suits he really enjoyed gold rings and necklaces. I really wasn't used to seeing a guy in his 40s wear that much jewelry, and sometimes caught myself staring at the rings during our sales meetings. His New York City accent was a little out of place upstate, but it was far from uncommon, and it gave him an edge.

I was thrilled to have a job, and they offered $10/ hour training for the first week and provided snacks. I decided I was really going to love this job. After all, I had never been in a real business or training meeting where we got paid to just sit there and listen or take notes. We wore ties and Sunday clothes and sat in fat leather swivel chairs around a huge table. There were pitchers of water and more math problems than I ever thought I would see outside of a college course. The difference was, if I learned this math, I'd keep getting paid. If I didn't learn it, I would be out. That ultimatum hit me after the third day of training when two of the other ten new hires weren't at the meeting, and Tony reminded us that we must be able to explain these financing options to customers with confidence or there was no need to come back to the dealership. Along with all of the math equations of trying to figure out discount percentages, profit margins and lease terminology, Tony taught us sales.

Tony put words to techniques I had been using for years in my own home as a middle child of five; negotiations, settlements, upselling a junky toy in trade for a better toy. Tony taught us negotiating 101, and he was a master. I watched him smile as he effortlessly talked people into spending thousands more than they planned. I watched him control buyers who didn't want to talk to anyone. Tony was a master at what he did, and I was a little awestruck by his abilities. Tony was a consummate salesman, and the things he taught me about working with people I have never forgotten.

He used to write a sales technique on the whiteboard in the morning and challenge us to add it to our interactions that day. "*Salesmanship is about control, not winning or losing*." Get control of your clients, and you never have to worry about winning. Selling a car or a widget uses the same skill set. Know the product you are selling because that knowledge provides you a sense of comfort when answering questions. Know the clients wants and needs. That means getting to know them by asking questions. Questions to the client and about the client will compel the client to answer. Most people love to talk about themselves, but you have to ask them first. Once you get them talking about themselves, they become much easier to control because they develop a sense of comfort and ease with you and will soon treat you like an old friend they haven't seen in a while. When you ask questions that develop rapport and foster that sense of ease, they will eventually trust you when you suggest that they might feel happier with the more expensive model car than the one they came in for. If you were "*just*" a salesperson, suggesting an extra $5000 would likely make them angry or cause them to leave the dealership, but since you are now friends, the upsell isn't nearly as risky. If you get good at your craft clients might actually believe you are suggesting the more expensive car for their needs and not your own. This may seem manipulative - and maybe it is. Nevertheless, this is how it often works.

One particular whiteboard challenge offered a $20 bill as a reward at the end of the day. Tony wanted to see who could get their clients to follow them around the dealership the longest. Unlike today's buyers who often arrive at the dealership with information they've gathered online, the early 1990s car buyers needed to go to the dealership for information. They needed to look at different makes and models to determine which car they were going to buy. There were days when customers would require a full walk around and test drive of more than ten cars before they would say something like, "*We are going to go home and think about it.*" That, of course, was infuriating because even the "green-pea" salesperson like me knew they were going to shop my prices to dealers and likely never come back. After spending two hours with these kinds of buyers on a Saturday morning, the dealer down the street could beat my price by $100 within ten minutes of being there and the customer would drive away in his car. It doesn't take too many of those types of encounters before Tony would give us the "*goodbye box.*"

The goodbye box was a literal cardboard box that once housed reams of paper that sat in the manager's office with the word "*Goodbye*" written on all four sides and the lid. Salespeople were encouraged to bring in family photos and small desk trinkets and awards they earned in the business and have them visible around their desk or work area. It helped customers see that salespeople were real people with families to provide for, making it a little harder to say no when the closing questions were asked. If a salesperson came into the dealership to start the workday and the goodbye box was on their desk there was nothing else to say. They were simply expected to pack up their trinkets and photos and leave. I saw those goodbye boxes dropped on many people's desks in the two years I was there. At first it was disturbing, but like all other kind of "*low dose trauma*" you get used to it. Before long we could actually joke about it when we saw it on someone's desk. They simply couldn't cut it. It was the way it was.

One of the many lessons I have learned and carried with me for over twenty years is you can't let the buyer walk. Yes, the buyer may be lying and yes, they might want to leave, but the statistics in 1992 stated that less than 10% of car buyers who leave a dealership without a contract will actually come back and buy from the salesperson. That lesson was drilled into us and we honed our salesmanship to a razor's edge in order to keep people from leaving without buying a car.

My wedding anniversary was coming up and my wife and I virtually had no money. I saw that $20 bill taped to the whiteboard in Tony's office from my desk and was determined to win it. Getting a total stranger to literally follow you around isn't hard if they want what you are leading them to, but if they are following you around and they don't even know why then you have developed a skill that not many people can master. I won the $20 that day and bought some flowers for my bride. The people that followed me came in to test-drive a Honda Civic. Three hours later they left with that Civic, in a color they didn't really like. After they drove the car and we determined we didn't have the color they wanted, they followed me to the lot and we looked at every other color Civic imaginable. With that $20 in mind, I showed them the business office, the repair shop, the body shop, the back lot where the cars are dropped off and the mechanics' lunchroom. I asked them questions and then started to walk away as they answered and they kept following. When they asked me questions I reciprocated, and they kept following. This might seem manipulative, rude or "*old school sleazy car salesman,*" but I merely worked the techniques Tony had taught me. People want you to know and care about their lives. If you ask them enough questions, they will literally follow you to make sure you know their answers.

Tony said questions were the key to everything in sales. The only time a client or a buyer would really "*win*" is when they were strong enough to not answer questions. No questions equals no answers equals no conversation equals no rapport, which almost always equals no sale. Later in my career I would come across a sales trainer who was literally a master of questions. His training and consulting business is all based on asking questions. It really does work.

Tony taught me many of the little techniques all good sales people know. When you make an offer or present a price, look the person in the eyes and smile. Don't flinch. Don't look away. The first one to talk loses. The first one to look away, loses. Present offers with confidence and make it clear that your offer is a win-win for both of you. Don't let numbers define what your win is. If you are selling a car at full price and everyone else that buys is getting a $2,000 discount is that wrong? No! The buyer is still getting a great car at the suggested price. That's the truth. Look them in the eye and know that you presented them a good price for a great deal. The fact is, it's only an overactive sense of "*fairness*" that puts doubt in your mind. It's that sense of fairness that says "*you're ripping them off*" when they paid what the sticker says the car is worth. I learned to be confident when I presented full price offers, and eventually it paid off and I began to sell a lot of cars.

The truth is, the happiest customers I ever had paid full or close to full price for their cars. They referred others to me and often bought more cars with me. The most bitter, angry, difficult customers were always the ones who tried to grind me down to the bottom of the profit margin and then still complained about the process. I quickly learned those people were never going to be satisfied because they cannot allow themselves to be happy. They tend to never feel like they just won and they often feel entitled to a better deal. I learned to avoid those people and, if I happened to be working with them, I would often choose to pass them to another salesperson. They will suck the happiness out of you, attract more negativity and are not worth your time investment.

To this day, I believe the Honda Accord is worth every penny of the sticker price, despite the fact that I will never pay that myself. Because I believe that, I could sell those cars today. This leads me to one of the greatest things Tony ever taught me: "*It's easy to sell to others that which you believe to be true*." That statement of fact and the way I internalized it throughout my life has cost me customers as well as jobs, but it has also made me a lot of money and provided a vital guidepost in my career.

Can I sell something I don't believe in? Yes, I can. Have I sold customers things I don't believe in? Sure, when times were tough, I would have done almost anything to provide for my family. Will I ever feel comfortable selling something I don't believe in? No, never. Fortunately I am at a place in may career where I don't have to compromise my personal sense of right or wrong to provide for my family. I also don't judge those who, like myself, may have had to do what they felt was necessary, at times, to make ends meet. But there is an inherent danger in doing that for too long. That danger is the methodical dulling of your sense of right and wrong.

Often salespeople are pulled into sales positions and paid exorbitant amounts of money to keep selling something that doesn't work or is bad for people. Trading your sense of self for a big paycheck can become a habit and before you know it, you're behaving like one of those people you used to dread talking to. If you get anything here, get this. It's hard enough on most of us to forgive ourselves for the past wrongs we might have done. If you are in a sales position right now that makes you feel bad about yourself or is bad for your customers, then do yourself a favor and quit that job as soon as you can. I know for a fact that a happy person doesn't have to fake being happy, and they can always sell more "*widgets*" when they feel good about themselves than when they don't. So save your self esteem and move to a sales position you can feel proud of.

Tony was a great trainer but ultimately he didn't see eye to eye with management on things like inventory management and compensating the sales force. I remember clearly seeing the "*goodbye box*" on his desk one morning. I don't know where he is today or what he is doing, but I will always be grateful for the lessons he taught me.

As I mentioned, a happy salesperson is a better salesperson and ultimately I knew I couldn't keep selling cars. I believed in the product and I was making good money, but I couldn't get past the stigma. Telling people I sold cars was not something I wanted to mention at parties. I honestly don't know if it has the same stigma today as it did in the 80s and 90s, but car salesmen were ranked below attorneys on the list of people we most dreaded talking to. I wanted to work at something I could be proud of, and while I was proud of my performance, I soon realized I had outgrown it and it was no longer fulfilling. I am not knocking the car salespeople who might be reading this because I believe it is a vital part of our economy, and to this day I prefer to buy a car from a professional. But internally, I was struggling with it and one day as I sat there wondering why my four-year degree was useless to me, I decided the only way I was going to get out of car sales was to use my experience to find an "*outside sales*" position.

I called it "*graduation day*" when I left the dealership for an outside sales position that paid me less money, took more hours per week and required far greater organizations skills. Sometimes you have to take a step back to make strides forward in your sales career. You have to refuse to be afraid to try just because the money is a little less or it might require more time. If the voice in your head says "*go for it*" then sometimes you have to do just that.

You have likely heard it said that fear causes more failures than trying will ever cause. It's true. I have tried many sales careers. Some have been failures. But the fact that I stepped out of my comfort zone and tried it is always something I am proud of to this day. That is a trait I tried desperately to convey to my three sons. I refused to discipline them for trying and failing at anything whether it was a sport or a job. I never wanted to hear them say they didn't try because they were afraid they would fail. It's important to step out and make that career move you have been thinking about, or call that prospect you talked to a while back and forgot to follow up with. Fear says they won't want to talk to you. Fear says you don't want to hear they bought from someone else. If you let fear win, you will surely fail. The only way to defeat fear is to do exactly the thing you feel afraid to do.

I have trained many sales people over the years and the number one predictor of failure in any sales office is the percentage of salespeople who are afraid of some aspect of their job. If you are afraid to call people on the phone, then start calling people on the phone and break that fear. If you are afraid to talk to strangers, then start talking to strangers and break that fear. Afraid to speak in public? Stand up and speak. Afraid to look people in the eye? Look them in the eye. You will always fail at what you fail to try. Once you start breaking these fears, you are on the road to a strong sales career. You can begin developing the techniques Tony taught until they become second nature.

Sales professionals have developed those techniques to a degree that they become more than second nature. They actually become a part of one's personality. Professional salespeople are actually some of the most enjoyable people to be around (if I do say so myself). Seasoned professionals can converse with nearly anyone at any time and about almost any subject. There is no real fear in their minds that they won't know what to say to people and their conversations aren't forced. That is a key difference between newer salespeople and the veteran; the newer, younger salespeople don't have the lifelong tales and conversational history in their repertoire yet.

You can't really shortcut that life experience. I have been to hundreds of conventions, and the salespeople I have met over the years have been hilariously funny with great personalities and a sense of style and confidence that attracts others. The people I know in sales aren't sleazy or creepy, manipulative or pushy. The true professionals have matured to a place where they know that sometimes they are going to lose, but most of the time they will win. Maturity for many seasoned salespeople has redefined their sense of winning. I know it has for me. Compromise is often the best outcome and my sense of victory comes when the compromise leans in my favor.

Outside sales was not only a graduation for me, it was a breakthrough. I was forced to develop a budget, a schedule, and expenditure and mileage sheets. It was a career, and I was getting good at it. The professional salesperson develops a sense of self confidence over time. I certainly did. Of course, it's great when your success is recognized by your peers or by a raise but that doesn't always happen. If you are waiting for those accolades to make you feel better about yourself, I suggest you find some other way to build yourself up. The company I worked for didn't do awards or substantial raises. I was challenged and I enjoyed my position but was always looking for more. I challenged myself to beat the sales numbers of the other salesmen. I tried to increase the volume sold in my territory every year. I tried to sell more while reducing expenses, and I was succeeding at all of those. Of course as any outside sales pro can tell you, this is exactly what the company wanted me to do. I was successful, but not happy. I had a company car, an expense account, travel, good customers and a decent income, but I was unfulfilled. I would make suggestions to management that went unheard. I would volunteer for leadership opportunities, but they were denied. And when I suggested a better way to develop new business I was harshly rebuffed. Back then I was reading Steven Covey and his 7 Habits as well as John Maxwell's Laws of Leadership. I soon knew for certain, that after four years of success, I wanted more. I wanted to be a part of something greater than myself. In the eight person sales force I was in, the next newest rep had eighteen years seniority on me. I had to realize that I wasn't headed anywhere in that position.

I knew that feeling all too well. After all, I had lived with it most of my life.

My father spent his entire career in an office. His goal was to slowly move up the ladder from entry level to middle management, praying for those tiny annual salary increases to continue and a promise of a retirement gift and a mediocre pension after thirty years. A plaque on the wall of his 18th floor office read, "*Doing a great job around here is like wetting your pants in a dark suit. You get a warm feeling inside, but nobody really notices.*" I will never forget that. He hated his job, but never dared to try something new. He never risked doing what he really wanted to do in life. Year after year I watched Dad come home from work after a 50+ mile drive each way. He was tired from the commute and exhausted by the job. I couldn't imagine working like that today ... to be 50 years old and feel 65 ... to literally hate going to work for the better part of a 30 year career. Why? Why would anyone do that? Was it fear that drove that behavior? Was it a sense of security knowing if he just plugged along his family would have food on the table? For years I was very proud of him for sticking with it. For sacrificing his "*dreams*" for this horrible civil servant position in the lower-middle levels of state government. Even so, I knew that kind of life wasn't for me.

I left my outside sales position, packed up my family and moved to Michigan for the chance to work for a great international company as an outside representative. Moving a family is tough, and it takes courage to do so. The courage I mean is that of my wife and family. In my mind, I was confident that I could do anything I put my mind to, and I had developed into a strong sales professional. Quoting one of America's most well-known outside sales professionals and one of my favorite movies of all time, Tommy Boy, I really did believe that I could "sell a ketchup popsicle to a woman in white gloves". Even though my wife believed wholeheartedly in my abilities, I never really gave her the opportunity to get behind the multi-state move. A true professional moves forward with confidence and a degree of moxy for sure, but you have to remember your spouse is not in your head with you. They need to be 100% convinced that the move is right or you will experience strife. Strife is the enemy of joy and joy is the key to a prosperous sales career.

We made it through that period because of our belief in God and my wife's strength. I remember thinking about the years growing up in the 1970s when my mom didn't work and my dad's job was still sucking the life out of him. Why didn't he move? We lived in a house that was over a hundred years old. His drive to work was over an hour each way and we had no money. We drank powdered milk and ate government cheese. Why didn't he move? My best clothes were hand-me-downs from my aunt, and my older brother was embarrassed to wear his to school. Why didn't he move?

I never got a straight answer from him the day I asked him those questions, but I don't really know if I needed to get the answer. My dad was a proud man and, like most people on this planet, he was just as afraid to fail as any of us. His generation saw his willingness to stick with the horrible job for that long as "strength." I don't see it that way. I am certain as I reflect on those years that much of what I saw him endure had a lasting effect on me. The fear of "not having" something like a job, food, or even a nice car can be a powerful motivator for sure. It can force people to play it safe like my dad did. It can also propel you to take risks with your career and your family like it did me.

After he died I was going through old photos of my dad at work smiling at parties and laughing with coworkers. I realized he might have hated his career, but not necessarily his job. He didn't take risks with his job and retired with a $32,000 per year pension and Social Security and he was content with that. "Rich" wasn't a term he ever personally experienced. A few years before he died, I told him I made more than $100,000 dollars a year. At first he didn't believe it, but then exclaimed, "*You're rich!*" I told him I was rich, but it had nothing to do with my income. My wealth is in my family and the legacy I leave my sons and grandchildren. I still believe that.

When you find a career path you love, whether in sales or not, find a way to stick with it. Jumping the fence for greener pastures is seldom the right choice when done hastily. When I left those companies, I liked what I was doing at the time, but I didn't love it and I didnt love who I was working for. I'm sure it's a goal of most people to find something they love and get paid to do it. A career is something you need to love if it is going to last. Like a marriage, a career will have ups and downs, good years and bad. If you are tempted to leave a job you have loved because it's been a tough year, stop and reflect on where you have been. Why did you love it in the first place? Are the reasons you are unhappy now permanent or temporary? You may need to ask yourself if your recent negativity is attracting more negativity? If you have any doubts, commit ninety days and bring as much positivity to your life and career as you can muster. Focus on making the people around you better and happier. If nothing changes, then it's likely time to find that greener pasture.

The first time I was fired from a sales position I was devastated. I felt like a failure on nuclear scale. I thought I was doing so well. My commissions were great, my optimism and drive were on full power, and I let my family and friends know how awesome everything was going in my business life. Then I had to try to explain to them what happened without fully understanding it all myself. Downsizing, management changes and market shifts are the enemies of sales people. They can sneak up on you and blindside your career without your even knowing they were there. They hurt at first, but in reality, aren't always your fault.

When my business took a major hit during 2008-2010, and I had to shut it down and sell my assets just to pay my bills, you can bet I was disillusioned. I was calling every person and business who owed me money, trying to collect. Like millions of other professionals around the world, I was beginning to panic. I forgot everything I know about sales, management and attitudes. When my company failed, I failed with it and ended up bouncing from ridiculous pursuit to ridiculous pursuit. There was no peace to be found. I had forgotten the lessons I had learned over the years. I had ignored the things that brought positivity to my life and, even though I was once again working and had an income, I wasn't thankful. I let strife in and there was no joy in what I was doing.

I truly believe that without joy there cannot be lasting success, but I had forgotten that. Instead, I jumped from sales job to sales job, knowing I was far more qualified to do the job than the people I was working for and longing for the day of independence I had come to love.

A sales professional is often getting recruited by businesses who want someone who is trainable, but seasoned ... someone they don't need to train in the basics, but is a fast learner with some street smarts and the ability to read people and situations. I found myself getting pulled into more "*promising*" opportunities and companies with a higher ceiling in their commission structure. I was never afraid to try something new, study something new, work in a new field, meet new people and take on new challenges. This is not necessarily the ideal life for many professionals or their families, but it offered me a dose of short-term excitement that I seemed to be craving. Sitting still in business was not a posture I wanted to take, and I am a firm believer in the adage that "comfortable can be the enemy of great." So I went back to selling 101 and began again.

A Word of Encouragement

When I train new salespeople I tell them that thick-skinned animals are the toughest to kill. Life will throw them a curveball or two, every salesperson needs to know that. That's how veteran sales people become "*thick skinned*" by taking a few of those curve balls on the chin. They learn to adapt their sales styles and techniques to fit the product or service they are marketing. Whether you are embarking on this most rewarding career or you are the wily old veteran, your ability to glean from others, continually learn, and be willing to adapt to change will ultimately determine the level of success and joy you will achieve.

In sales, "*success*" is often a moving target. What is considered success in your market today is frequently considered mediocre performance tomorrow. Developing a "*thick skin*" is paramount to a sales person. The thin-skinned vulnerable salesperson is not likely to remain a salesperson because they can't take criticism and have a fear of failure. If you can sit through a sales meeting, where you are getting lectured by a manager about missed sales goals that were set for you instead of by you, and then go out and do your job to the best of your ability, you are becoming a professional. Many people can't endure that, but it's the difference between success and failure.

Having a thick skin is an asset to the professional. Being able to smile through adversity and generate optimism and joy when the sales numbers are slumping are key signals that you have become a true professional. Always continue to find reasons to generate joy and positivity in your sales office, even if that office is the front seat of your car. It's easy to be a whiner. It's easy to get together with other sales people and complain about how poorly management is functioning. It's more difficult to remain that beacon of joy in your office, but ultimately it will be better for you and your income. If you find yourself being a negative person be prepared for a paradigm shift brought on by a management ultimatum, which could be the equivalent of Tony's Goodbye Box.

We are all human and we all make mistakes from time to time. That's why I encourage you as you progress through your career to never stop building your network. You never know when you may have to lean on them after a paradigm shift. I could get fired tomorrow and I would be able to set up referral lunches with a dozen or more people the next day. Although there's no guarantee I would get hired, I would have a good place to start.

Slumping sales numbers can end a job, but don't let them end your career if it's a career you love. A professional salesperson needs to release that pain of loss and fear of failure and move on quickly. Like a mechanic with their own tool chest, a salesperson has a set of well-developed tools that are marketable in many companies and in many different industries. Trust your training, trust your abilities, and learn to believe in your own professional success. I learned the hard way that it is difficult to explain to the people who are not in sales how you can be "*successful*" in your position and still lose your job. Remaining humble is the best policy. Sales people like to get together and tell tall tales of "*big fish*" and exaggerated incomes; it's better to just shut up stay humble and continue to hustle.

From industry to industry, company to company, the business cards I have collected and relationships I have fostered have developed into a powerful network of executives and colleagues who understand what makes a professional salesperson. That kind of network takes years for most people to develop. Once I realized I never wanted to leave the outside sales world, staying focused on personal growth and business prowess became paramount. Protecting your network is also important. Remember, these contacts and relationships you have made over the years are yours. If you work for a company that demands full access to the leads or relationships you have made while working for them, then by all means hand them over if you feel you need to be employed. These companies require you to hand over the contacts and sales leads you have made while under their employment. I do suggest keeping a copy of that information for yourself of course.

For nearly a quarter century I have been in outside sales. I have worked for great people and bad people. I have worked with crooks and saints. I have studied hard and taught many. I have sold everything from cutlery to condominiums, hand soaps to golf courses. Through it all one thing continues to surface for me. I love providing something someone wants (or needs) to people.

Today, real estate has become my passion. It is without a doubt the most satisfying sales position I have ever had. There is a peace I feel when providing this service to someone who needs my help. I love the excitement, variety and the sense of accomplishment from this career field. I am an independent contractor with a history of building relationships and marketing products for businesses. Now, I provide a vital service for extraordinary people. I market their properties in ways they didn't know could be done. I am a solver of problems, and I help make their dreams come true.

If I am honest with myself my career choices have always been about providing for my family and doing something I really enjoy. I was further blessed if that path glorified God, but He was not always the priority. Now, I have finally attained a position that I believe does all three of those things, and I never want it to end.

I have heard it said that "*we are the sum total of our life experiences*" and there is some validity to that. Perhaps it's more accurate to say that we are the "*sum total of the decisions we make.*" Our decisions become our direction, for better or worse. It's clear to me now that Joy = Success and Success = Joy. I did not always understand that. I believe that true success is finding joy in the journey and not hoping to find it in some theoretical destination. Success and joy in your business will attract more success and joy to your business and life.

What's really amazing to me is the fact that we all have the choice to be successful or not. It's true. I choose to be happy and joyful even when I don't "*feel it*" due to temporary circumstances. Choosing joy will bring success, and I can assure you that success has surely delivered me more joy in my current career path than I have ever known before. Here's wishing you and abundance of joy no matter what your circumstances or next step you take on your individual journey.

Geoffrey A. Brown | Bio

Geoff was born in Western New York and grew up the middle child of five. This is where he credits his early abilities to read people and negotiate for mutually beneficial outcomes. "*There are few more demanding crucibles of negotiation in the world than arguing for your one-in-seven chance to use the single bathroom in your family's farmhouse*," he says.

Geoff has made a career in sales and marketing of products and services for nearly 30 years. He has been married to Virginia "*Ginger*" Brown for 27 years, whom he calls the "*solid rock*" of his career and life. Together, they have three sons: Nicholas, Daniel and Nathan. "*Ginger never doubted my ability to provide for our family*," he says. "*She reminds me of that when I lose sight of the end game for short term accolades.*"

Geoff's professional sales career started in college selling cutlery, along with first-generation cell phones. He has been successful selling everything from school buses to commercial glazing to industrial tooling supplies. Although Geoff has been a business owner, entrepreneur and business partner in several small companies, he believes he has finally found the perfect niche for his well-developed skill set.

"*Real estate has provided the perfect market, method and demographic for the abilities I have developed over my career. It has allowed me to provide a life-changing service to people who need my expertise. It has also allowed me to build a business model that highlights my strengths, downplays my weaknesses and yet still conforms to the professional licensure guidelines,*" he says. "*In short, real estate service lets me earn a great living doing exactly what I like to do, when and where I want to do it. My career in real estate has allowed me to be me, and I have never felt more joy in my career.*"

CHAPTER 3

From a Small Town, To a Big Dream

By Kevin Kuch

My journey started off in the small town of Peterborough, Ontario, Canada where I grew up in a loving family of five. My Dad was a sheet metal worker and my Mom was a homemaker and ran a daycare out of the house. The oldest sibling in the family was my brother Jason and the youngest was my Sister Audra. We didn't have a lot of money, but we always had what we needed to live comfortably. We had food in our stomachs, a roof over our heads, clothes on our backs, a bed to sleep in at night and lots of love in the household. They were things I never thought about when I was younger, but certainly see the value in today as an adult.

My parents were always able to make it work. My Dad would work full time hours and also pick up overtime when he could, to bring in extra money. My Dad would also ride his bike to work if my Mom needed the car for grocery shopping or appointments. Both of them were committed to doing their part and everything just seemed to fall into place.

Having an older brother and a younger sister, I was the proverbial middle child. My brother typically had my parent's attention as the first-born and my younger sister was the only girl and was therefore the apple of my Fathers eye and my Mom's "*baby girl*". Some might say a lot about the middle child, but for me, I enjoyed not having eye's on me for the most part. As a result of less attention, I managed to get myself into some trouble from time to time. I was extremely outgoing and curious, but more of that later in my story.

Up to the age of 15, I lived with my family in Ontario housing, which was government assisted living. We lived in a small semi-detached house in the south end of Peterborough. I remember some of my friend's parents owning their homes and I always thought about how amazing that must have been. Even at a young age I could see the value in owning your own home. As luck would have it, we came into some money when I was 15. Ok, the luck was actually bad, as my Mom was in a serious car accident and was provided a financial settlement. Fortunately however, that was enough to get us a down payment for a house. Once my Mom was healed enough to start the search, we started looking for our home. We found a nice raised bungalow on the hill in the south end that allowed us to go to the same schools and not be too far from the neighborhood that we were familiar with. For me, that was heaven.

Unfortunately, that heavenly moment didn't last. My Dad now being a homeowner didn't want anybody else's kids in the house. To provide a little more context, on top of my Mother's babysitting, my parents had also been foster parents to approximately 40 kids over the course of 15 years. Now that's a lot of wear and tear on a house and I could totally see my Dad's point. My Mom not prepared to do anything other than her passion of caring for children, was at a loss. It was that challenge that showed me how strong my Mom really was at the time. At the age of 44, my Mom went back to high school to get her Grade 12 diploma. After achieving her grade 12 diploma, she continued on with her schooling by going to College to study nursing. One event that I will never forget in my life, is graduating College the same year as my Mom; truly a proud moment for both of us. That was my first lesson in persistence and my teacher was my very own Mother.

Even though my Mom was successful with gaining a new skill and now working as a Registered Practical Nurse, she was still not happy working outside of the home. Unfortunately at that time, my Dad had lost his job of 25 years from the sheet metal plant and was now unemployed. With Mom unhappy and wanting to work with kids at home and Dad not knowing how to find another job in the small town with limited work, the bills started to pile up. Did I mention that my Brother and I were also eating everything in sight? Yes, bills pilling up! For the first time in my life, I truly experienced stress and unhappiness.

For two and half years we stayed in that house on the hill surrounded by financial stress, arguing and a feeling of lack in the world. They were very trying times for all of us. I remember feeling that I would have to find a way to make as much money as I could, just in case. I actually went to the welfare office to ask how I could qualify for welfare and get my own apartment. I was politely told that I was too young to qualify and that I was lucky to have a home already. My thought was that if I had a roof over my head, I would be able to take my family in if things got worse. Not discouraged though, I also started working three jobs and banking every penny that I could in my savings account. I would work a security shift at the mall, followed by a maintenance shift at the mall and then work at a local restaurant on weekends either bussing tables or bartending. I was determined to make and save as much money as I could. My first lesson on persistence was getting actioned.

Then it happened; the dream of owning our own home crashed suddenly when the bank, after several attempts to collect mounting mortgage payments, repossessed our house. At that point, our family broke apart and scattered. My Mom rented an apartment while going on welfare and took me in. My Dad managed to find another job, so he rented a house and took my Sister in and my Brother moved in with some friends. How things had changed from a loving, peaceful household, to a dream come true that shattered after only two and half years. It was a shock to all of us. It was at that time that I vowed, this will never happen to me again. At the age of 17, I knew I would have to start doing things differently then what I saw my parents doing. It was also at that time that I anchored a terrible fear of loss and a poor relationship with money, that was again, coupled with the fear of loss.

As much as I inherited a strong work ethic from both of my parents, the challenge for me was that I had absolutely no passion for school or learning in a structured environment. There were countless times over the years that I would skip school and get into mischief. Skipping to go swimming, or shoplifting, or even breaking and entering into an abandoned house to see how much damage I could do. I was a free spirit and unless I could see a reason not to do something, I was all in! After a few run-ins with the law and a few physical scars from thoughtless actions, I started thinking to myself that there must be a "smarter" way to live. As much as I knew that I had to "*do things differently*", I didn't know what that meant. There I was, a bad student, with no love lost from my teachers, no direction in life and living in an apartment on welfare with my Mom.

All I could think to do was to make money at my jobs and save as much as I could. I even went to the bank to ask how I could make more interest on my money than what was currently being provided by my savings account. I was instructed to invest in T-Bills, which were secured by the government and paid slightly more in interest than a savings account. T-Bills made sense to me for two reasons; one, they were safe and two, they paid more interest than a savings account. That was my first experience with investing and understanding that my money could actually make me money. I also saw how my Mom went back to school and learned a craft that allowed her to start a career. Realizing that bussing tables and working part time jobs was not going to get me the life and security I wanted, I begrudgingly decided to go to college. Now working three jobs and going to college full time, I was determined to gain financial security and make a life for myself.

After completing college I found full time employment in the field that I studied, Telecommunications. I worked for a small Interconnect company in Peterborough for a few months, until one day I was laid off due to a lack of work. With a small shop like that one, it was common to reduce manpower when the work was slow. Luckily for me, about a week after I was laid off, the owner landed another big contract and I was back on again. Well, that only lasted three weeks and again, as the low man on the pole, I was laid off yet again. Discouraged, I started looking for other work. Fortunately I found work at a pasta sauce factory. Not exactly my passion, but it paid the bills. Then, as luck would have it, there was another layoff and it just happened to be the shift that I was on. At that point, I had enough of small town living and decided to look for an area with more opportunity.

Further motivation for me at the time was the fact that I had started dating a girl and we were getting serious. It was now her and I that had to start planning how our life would turn out. At the age of 21, we decided to get married and then shortly after that leave Peterborough, which up to that point was the only life I knew. I found an apartment in Guelph, ON, about two hours from Peterborough on the west side of Toronto. I skipped right over Toronto because I preferred the idea of smaller town living. The difference between Guelph and Peterborough however, was that Guelph and the surrounding areas actually had more opportunity.

My life from the age of 19 seemed to run in major events every two years. I got engaged at 19, married at 21 and moved away, bought a house at 23, had my Daughter at 25, my Son at 27 and sadly, separated at 29 and divorced at 31. So many significant events packed into a 12-year span. Ok numerology fanatics, have fun with that one!

I realized after the demise of my marriage and breakup of my own family, that I was so driven to survive and never relive my broken past, that I never nurtured myself or my marriage. I was so focused on work and providing security for my family, that my plan backfired and again, I felt like I had lost everything. As much as I had managed to buy and keep a house, I still ended up with a broken family and ultimately lost my house through the divorce. That was a more painful lesson than the first one. The lesson here for me was that I needed to care for myself first, so that I would be healthy enough to care for others.

My focus now was to keep a strong relationship with my kids and to finally focus on my own personal health. I knew that I had to grow emotionally, I had to re-define my relationship with money and I had to stop thinking in terms of lack. My search was on for a better me. I started thinking about what made me happy as a child. My thought was that I did a lot of interior camping with the scouts when I was younger and I remembered that I really loved being in nature. During a conversation with a co-worker while talking about my marriage breakup, my co-worker suggested that I back pack across Europe to "*find myself*". Not wanting to be away from my kids, I politely suggested that that wouldn't work for me. The conversation then went to backpacking in Killarney, a Provincial Park here in Ontario. He had mentioned to me that he had gone with friends the last couple of years, but the friends he went with had to bow out this year. That was it, I could get away for a few days with friends and start the journey of looking after myself. We managed to find a third person to go with us and I'm happy to say that the group has grown and we have been going on the same trip now for 12 years. Along with camping I also started roller blading, golfing and playing the piano. Now learning to have fun again in my life, I figured I needed to start working on my relationship with money and my emotional health in general.

What hasn't been mentioned, is that even though I was learning to have fun again, I was crying and depressed nearly every night and most days at work, from separation from my kids. I was a very active Father and to not see my kids every day was a greater loss than my houses. While going through all of this, I decided that I needed to look for answers outside of my own circle of friends and my own reading. I felt that I needed to start seeing a counsellor that didn't resemble a buddy at the other end of a beer bottle. I started searching for councillors and when I found options, I started binge counselling, if that's even a thing. I started seeing a one on one councillor and I was going to group therapy sessions as well. My counselling led me to some peace about my loss and started to build my confidence and sense of self-worth. I continued to go to counselling to work on myself and would then go out with friends, when I didn't have my kids, to nurture my relationships and try to again "find myself" as they say. Then when I had my kids, the rest of the world didn't exist.

Through going out with some newfound friends, I ended up meeting a women. We dated for some time and then decided to move in together. Let's just say she passed the test when she knew that nothing was going to come between me and my kids. She not only respected that, she has supported that to this day and has actually enriched all of our lives in a way that only a women with such a heart can do. Naturally I married her and my second chance at a relationship was born.

As much as my life seemed to be getting back on track, I still had a poor relationship with money. It wasn't that I didn't have enough to live on with my current job, it was that I was in constant fear of losing it and everything that I had worked for. It was in the next few years that I really started to look for yet again, a better way. I started reading incessantly, looking for distinctions on how to become successful and happy in life. My wife and I would read in bed every night and shared things that we were learning. One night my wife asked me to let me know when she could interject on my reading and share something with me. I came to a break in my book and I set it down, ready to listen to her next found insight. She read a section to me out of Robert Kiyosaki's book, *Rich Dad Poor Dad*. She read about the difference between an asset and a liability. I could not believe what I had just heard. I was floored to think that I was in my mid-thirties and I didn't own any assets, or for that matter, I didn't truly know the difference between an asset and a liability. I knew that the information she had just shared, was life changing.

In the days following that bedtime discussion, I remember driving my kids to school one morning and hearing on the radio that the *Rich Dad Poor Dad* team was going to be giving a seminar in Kitchener on a weekend coming soon. After dropping the kids off at school, I pulled into a parking lot and called my wife. I asked her to go online and get us tickets to the event. Without hesitation, she secured us two tickets to the event. The weekend came and like the book, it was another life changer. It was a course packed full of insights and distinctions that simply made sense to me and left me wanting more.

After attending the event, we were offered more courses. Having gone through an expensive divorce, losing money on a house during the divorce, child support payments and a destination wedding, I was faced with the prospect of having to go further into debt for more education. The surprise to me was, that without hesitation, we both knew that it was the right thing to do. I was starting to do things differently in my life and taking an active role in my learning, my personal well-being and the health of my marriage, was helping me build a better and happier life.

Seeing the impact that one book and some training had on my life, gave me the motivation I needed to become an avid reader and lover of seminars. I started to read books aggressively, go on courses, watch online seminars, go to live seminars, always looking for those distinctions that would change my life. *Think and Grow Rich, As A Man Thinketh, Awaken The Giant Within, Cashflow Quadrant, The Four Hour Work Week*, were just some of the books that I started with. The material was life changing and I was now entering my days with anticipation of what could be, rather than apprehension for what might happen1. It was in the book *Think and Grow Rich* that I discovered that I was now using one of Napoleon Hill's success principles which was Personal Initiative. I was fully engaged and making things happen in my life.

There was however a negative side to gaining so many insights. I started to question everything around me and quickly realized that I wasn't living up to my full potential. I got uncomfortable with trading my time for money when I knew that my value far exceeded my paycheck. I lost interest in my job because I didn't like the feeling of working so hard, yet seeing the same result on my paycheck. I was producing greater and greater results, but as an employee, I was only paid for the job and the value that the job brought to the company. During this process of questioning, I started to reduce my work hours feeling as though I would only give the company the time that was equal to what they paid me for. I was down to an 8-hour work day and a 40-hour work week; no more 60 hour weeks for me. An honest day's work for an honest day's pay. Well, that back fired. With the Management team seeing my results pale in comparison to my previous results due to my self-imposed reduced work hours, I was quickly put on a Performance Improvement Plan (otherwise known as a PIP). It was a plan to get my work results back to an acceptable level, with a firm understanding that I would be terminated if I didn't comply. When I received the news from my Manager, I was shocked to say the least. I will say that I was thankful to have such a good relationship with my acting Manager at the time, as it made my next decision an easy one. I said to myself, this is a test, how will you pass it with grace and dignity? I took a deep breath, told myself to stay calm, acknowledged the PIP and said, ok, let's do this. Using another of Napoleon Hills Success Principles, I kept a Positive Mental Attitude. My manager and I put a plan together to "*get me back on track*". About the same time that I was put on the PIP, I was also provided a book by my Manager titled Good to Great. The books main concept was to get the right people on the bus, the wrong people off the bus and finally, the right people in the right seats before travelling to your destination. While studying my job intensely and ensuring that I was satisfying all of the performance markers of the PIP, I was also reading the book I was just given. I was provided an allotted time to complete the PIP and to the Management team's satisfaction and surprise, I completed the requirements in about half of the allotted time. Things were good again, for about a month.

This is where the story gets interesting. Shortly after completing the PIP and now having completed the newfound book, I made a decision. My decision was to quit my job and start my own company. I realized that I was not only in the wrong seat on the bus, but I was actually on the wrong bus. Wow, what a revelation! That experience really brought the old adage to life for me that life happens for you and not to you. Through the process of the PIP, I gained several new skills in the high tech world and better organized my time.

Through the book, I realized that I was not in the right place for my personality, my skills or my passion. The next stop on my journey was my own business where I could start to trade results for money, instead of time for money and really enjoy what I do.

I decided that the path of least resistance on the journey to self-employment, was to go with what I knew. I knew the world of Unified Communications and Data Networking with Bell Canada, the large Telecommunications company I had previously been employed by. I had over 20 years of experience with voice and data technologies that helped businesses communicate to the world and their strategic market. The problem was, my seat on the previous bus was as an Architect of the technologies in the Engineering department and I didn't know how to translate that into my own business. I always had a deep understanding of the technologies I worked on, however, I now classified myself as a people person with strong interpersonal skills and was ready to focus on relationships and not technology. Sales, that was my new direction. Having that realization was a little scary as I had never been in a sales role before. For some reason I felt that it was the right fit; my own business with me in a sales role. I guess you could say that I was now on a sales bus and in the driver's seat. Luckily for me, the company I had previously worked for, Bell Canada, had a Certified Sales Partner program. Having left the company on good terms, yes, I worked diligently on a succession plan for my previous position, I was accepted into the partner program without question. I was now exercising yet another of Napoleon Hill's Success Principle's, Faith. It was a huge leap of faith to leave a great paying job with benefits and a pension plan, to venture out on my own into a world of Sales that I knew little about.

It was July of 2015 that Strategy Global Inc was born, and I now had a definite purpose. My high tech sales and consulting business was now a reality and I was ready to trade my value for money. I organized my finances, got a website up and running, created a logo and did all of things I thought were required to get a business running. There was now one small problem; what the hell was Strategy Global Inc in the world of business. I was the new guy on the block and I had to start introducing myself.

The first Monday of my new life arrived and I was terrified. I would drive to the Bell offices in Mississauga to start introducing myself to the internal sales teams and when I arrived at the buildings, I would just sit in my car, panic stricken. Day after day, for two weeks, I drove to the parking lot, sat in my car and stared out the window. I had lost my identity and with the fear of not having my skills and value recognized, I was paralyzed. Then one day I got up the courage to actually go into the building. I walked into the building like I was running late for a meeting. I wanted anyone that saw me to think that I was rushing in for a meeting and that I didn't have time to talk; avoidance was the goal. I marched upstairs to the first little workroom I could find, went in, sat down and closed the door. I literally stayed in there for about five minutes and then hurried back to the car and went home. It took me about one more week of hiding in small meeting rooms to get the courage up to go all the way into the building sales floor to introduce my new company and the new me. The first day that I had fully immersed myself into the sales floor as the new me, an old friend of mine that worked on the floor saw me passing by and grabbed me to ask me some questions. He knew my technical strength and asked if I would work on an account with him. Of course I said yes and my first customer was born. We closed three contracts together that week and I officially classified myself as a sales person.

Now a Sales person with my own company, things are better right? Well, kind of. I maintained a great relationship with my wife and kids, business was slowly picking up and I was certainly feeling better about the bus I was on and the seat I was in. I felt that my counselling in the past was invaluable for dealing with grief and major change in my life, so I started to think about how I could find someone to help me plan a better future. A life coach, that's what I needed. It's amazing what you'll find when you know what to look for. I had recently watched a very good friend of mine hit rock bottom and nearly kill himself with drugs and alcohol. I watched as another good friend of his took him to a Life Coach who happened to be the friend's cousin. The short version is that I watched my friend go from rock bottom, to kicking drugs and alcohol, embrace a serious relationship, marriage, start a family and grow his business exponentially in less than two years. I had never witnessed such a drastic change in anyone. I was a believer. I started seeing the same Life Coach and to my amazement, she helped me broaden my thinking, change my perception of my world and further work through some feelings of guilt and loss that I apparently still harboured about my lost time with my kids. Another major lesson for me was that no one can do it alone. There are people out there that truly want to help and the sooner you look for the help you need, the sooner you will feel better and can then continue on the path to your life's purpose. One more lesson I'll pass on from my Life Coach is that you have to be gentle with yourself. You are doing the best you can with the knowledge that you have. As they say, you don't know what you don't know (Unknown author).

It is now three years later and my company is still going strong. I have grown my team to 8 partner companies and a third party order entry team that honestly, helps me look like a rock star and also helps me fill in the roles that I'm not overly good at, or enjoy. This was yet another lesson. I realized that if I focused on what I was good at, like connecting with people, figuring out complex solutions and making complex solutions simple and understandable, I could leverage other people with other strengths to have my brand, Strategy Global, bring more value to the marketplace. Napoleon Hill explains that a person cannot rise to success alone and that a Mastermind Alliance is necessary for the attainment of success.

Now feeling much happier than ever in my life, I am starting to focus on paying it forward. I have started going to charity events and looking for ways that I can help. My wife and I are developing courses to help entrepreneurs set goals and visions for their future. I do my best to coach my kids on living with an open mind, following their passion and working on the skill of focus, to succeed in whatever their heart desires.

My journey has brought me to a place that has taught me that first and foremost, you must commit to being an eternal student. We are here to learn and with the access to information today, learning can be easy and fun. If you don't like to read, download an audiobook and simply listen. If you don't like to listen, jump on YouTubeTM and watch the content. It has never been easier than it is today to get the material you need to change your life. If you are not already pushing yourself to learn everything you can to build a bigger and better you, it's time to start now.

To your success!

Author's note:

As I write the final edit to this chapter, I received a phone call from a friend that had informed me of the passing of the creator of Journey's to Success, Tom Cunningham. Tom was the person who inspired me to take a chance to write this chapter and share my story. Thank you Tom for the inspiration and you will always be remembered for all of the good you brought to this world. Thank you for the Love my friend and Rest in Peace.

Kevin Kuch | Bio

Kevin Donald Kuch is a Husband, a Father and a Canadian Businessman, currently living in Waterloo, ON, Canada.

Kevin was born in the small town of Peterborough, ON, located about an hour and half north east of Toronto, ON. Raised by loving parents and akin to an older brother and a younger sister, Kevin enjoyed growing up in a small town.

Kevin was educated at Sir Sandford Fleming College in his hometown of Peterborough, where he spent three years and received a diploma in Electronics Engineering, specializing in Telecommunications. Kevin started his career at a small interconnect company in Peterborough and later moved to Waterloo Region in 1996 to continue growing in his career.

Kevin is still in the Telecom industry today and currently owns and operates a high tech Sales and Consulting business named Strategy Global Inc, located in Waterloo Region. He Specializes in Unified Communications technologies as well as multi-site networking, and structured cabling.

Kevin has a passion for many things; among them are Family, Business, Music, Golf, Travelling, Reading and Writing.

Kevin's immediate family of five consists of his soulmate and wife Anmmarie and his two children from a previous marriage, Emily and Ethan. Let's not forget their lovable Springer Spaniel Mocha and that makes five. Kevin cherishes the opportunity to show Emily and Ethan a creative home driven by the passion for Entrepreneurship.

With business as Kevin's every day focus, he likes to unwind by strumming a guitar and singing or getting out on the golf course for some fresh air and exercise. Kevin has been playing the guitar for over twenty years and has been golfing for just as long. Kevin's always up for a great jam session or a challenging round of golf.

One of Kevin's aspirations is to circle the world. Since starting to travel in his mid-thirties with his wife Anmmarie, Kevin has caught the adventure bug and is determined to see the world. Already having been to many islands such as Sint Maarten, Cuba, Jamaica and Dominican Republic, he has also been to several US states and once across the Atlantic to France.

Kevin continues to expand his life through avid reading and writing and is looking forward to what the future has in store for him!

CHAPTER 4

Bach, Beethoven, Brahms and Bartok: Lessons from the Big Four

By Cyndi Vos, BMus, MEd

Walking into a conference room with Johann Sebastian Bach, Ludwig Van Beethoven, Johannes Brahms and Bela Bartok is an extremely educational and life-changing encounter if you are prepared to learn from some of the greatest salesmen history has to offer. What does music have to do with sales you ask? Let me tell you a story.

Our meeting was set for 10:00am for which I arrived 15 minutes early as I wanted to look prompt but not over eager. I sat in the waiting room and admired the various accolades on the wall showcasing the achievements of the Big Four. It was impressive. Each of them had their own wall, which was very intriguing. I looked at each wall and wondered why they decided to make a point of individualizing each wall and each individual person's accomplishments, rather than unite the team as a whole and interlock the achievements as a team.

Johann Sebastian walked out to greet me. I have to say. I stopped in my tracks and had to take a deep breath. He was so distinguished. He had a controlled proper charm that exuded authority and direction. The structure of preludes and fugues started to race through my mind instantly. The visual link of the true foundation of purpose flashed before my eyes and ran through my soul. As a child my first lessons in performance where based on the teachings of J. S. Bach and here he stood before me and greeted me as though we were friends with a true breadth of history.

We walked over to the wall that was dedicated to him and he asked me what I thought? I told him that I enjoyed reviewing the walls but did not understand the full purpose. He replied by saying that each wall defined each person as someone who is unique and the connecting of the walls showed how all of them were united and joining them together helped form a world of understanding.

Each wall held a picture of each man in the middle and under Bach's picture the words *Definiteness of Purpose* were printed on a plaque. I was familiar with this principle and I wanted to know how Bach had used it in his life and why had he chosen it as his label for his plaque. He ginned at my questioning and started by saying "*The aim and final end of all music should be none other than the glory of God and the refreshment of the soul.*" That is purpose to me.

Bach was always definite in his plans and created all of his works with a spirit of faith. He was a man that lead with integrity and believed in a sense of perfect harmony. You could see it in all of his ventures in music, work and life. Like to lead his team with a sound plan. He knew about in the power of teaching others.

We started to walk into the conference room and I asked him how did you determine your definiteness of purpose? He stopped for a moment and looked directly at me and said that everything is created out of a well-developed plan. He started each project with a concise statement created by sound harmonic structure and then let the melodic structure develop around solid principles. His final statement to me before we neared the entrance of the conference room was "*It's easy to play any musical instrument: all you have to do is touch the right key at the right time and the instrument will play itself.*"

I smiled and thought – if it was only that easy.

Just as we start to walk through the entrance I look up and see a plaque above the door with *Mastermind Alliance* as a title. The Big Four really knew how to make people feel welcome. I had not even entered the room yet I felt as though I was already a member of something that was so powerful. An alliance that could and would steer me into a focused direction with a team that could lead to me achievements that I had not yet even conceived.

I walk through the threshold and look across the room. And then I almost faint. I honestly had to put my hand on the table to steady myself. All I have to say is that what people say about Ludwig van Beethoven is true! Beethoven is so charismatic. The energy that shoots off that man is full of force. A force that is instantly intoxicating but intoxicating in such a positive energizing way.

Ludwig must be use to having this affect on people as he quickly moved toward me and gently grabbed my hand and helped steady me then welcomed me to room of perfect harmony.

I was introduced to Beethoven's work in my early teens and felt an instant connection with his compositions. All of them. His piano works came fairly easy to me and his lines of his orchestral works ran clear in my ears and my mind.

Beethoven built much of his work working with two or more melodies that worked actively together in perfect harmony toward a common definite objective. It was clear in his presentations that he felt no one mind was complete by itself. He had a knack of being able to find the right people who had the ability to do the job and create masterpieces he wished to create beyond words.

Being unsure of how to communicate with Beethoven I hesitated and looked down before I started with all the questions I had for him. When I looked up he reassured me that even though hearing words was a challenge for him his communication skills were stronger than anything that could be expressed by a typical conversation. Just as Bach had done he looked me in the eyes and told me to ask anything.

I spoke clear and precise and simply asked "*how do you do it?*"

"You ask me where I get my ideas. That I cannot tell you with certainty. They come unsummoned, directly, indirectly - I could seize them with my hands - out in the open air, in the woods, while walking, in the silence of the nights, at dawn, excited by moods which are translated by the poet into words, by me into tones that sound and roar and storm about me till I have set them down in notes."

When he finished his sentence, it felt as though I had just finished playing the first moment from his Sonata No. 14 in c# minor, better known as the Moonlight Sonata. I could see Beethoven sitting beside me with his head laying on the piano feeling the vibrations of the sound while watching my hands move through the notes. He had said exactly what I had hoped he would.

He continued on telling me that he directed his alliances with the 10 Basic Motives as a base – self preservation, love, fear, sex, desire for life after death, freedom for mind and body, anger, hate, desire for recognition and self expression and finally wealth. Beethoven used the power of the motives as he conducted his groups with clear unmistakable signals. He never wanted deafness to limit his ability to be creative and achieve his purpose. He had the ability to be a thinker and a leaper and was never afraid to draw on specialized skills of team members. You could see and feel that Beethoven worked hard to maintain confidence, understanding, courage, fairness and justice at all times. He knew that a strong mastermind gives you full access to everyone's spiritual power.

At the end of our conversation he thanked me for believing in him and to me that "*From the glow of enthusiasm I let the melody escape. I pursue it. Breathless I catch up with it. It flies again, it disappears, it plunges into a chaos of diverse emotions. I catch it again, I seize it, I embrace it with delight... I multiply it by modulations, and at last I triumph in the first theme. There is the whole symphony.*"

With those words I felt secure in our alliance and I thanked him for sharing his knowledge and passion with me. I knew from that moment forward that every time I needed the strength of a mastermind it would be there for me.

We took a 15-minute break and Bach said that he would go let Johannes Brahms know that I was ready for him. The third of the heavy hitters.

He sat at the table in a very specific place and in front of him was a stone that had the word *Faith* etched into it.

Brahms is the combination of a traditionalist and an innovator. This was evident as soon as he walked into the room. He was an academic with presence. He was also an academic with faith.

Like I said earlier, Brahms was a heavy hitter and without me even beginning to ask my first question he started with "*In my study I can lay my hand on the Bible in the pitch dark. All truly inspired ideas come from God. The powers from which all truly great composers like Mozart, Schubert, Bach and Beethoven drew their inspirations is the same power that enabled Jesus to do his miracles.*" My eye must have been extremely large as he finished with stating "The idea comes to me from outside of me - and is like a gift. I then take the idea and make it my own - that is where the skill lies." Then he winked and me and said "*To follow in Beethoven's footsteps transcends one's strength*." I was warned that he could start off a bit strong but would quickly become relatable when he felt a connection with his audience.

Brahms strength laid in his sense of faith and he knew that faith must be active. You cannot simply have faith; you must use it. He was in touch with the external world (deliberate organized intelligence) and the internal world (senses such as touch, sight, hearing, taste and smell). Brahms knew that one must find the source of energy and then put that energy and thoughts into action.

He asked me if I had ever played any of his pieces. My eyes filled with tears and I said one of my favourite pieces of all times was Rhapsody No.2 in g minor Op. 79. It was a song that I had learned for my fourth year of university. Initially it was for my graduation recital. However, it also was the song that I played for my grandfather just before he passed away and then again at his funeral. That song symbolized for me the union of academia and faith. My grandfather was so proud of me for what I was achieving in my career and I needed that faith that Brahms had created in that piece to help me get through one of the most difficult losses of my life. Through that piece I will always remain connected to my grandfather and I will forever be grateful to Brahms for creating that miracle.

We finished our discussion and we shook hands and I felt the warmth of my grandfather surround me.

Now I was on schedule for my final visit with the "*wild child*" of creativity. Mr. Bela Bartok. If there was an interesting rhythm to be written, coupled with combinations of folk tunes, sourced in an analytical twist, Bartok was your man.

Bartok was not short on imagination. This man was always pushing the envelope while trying to keep music in its simplest terms. He looked for the beauty in the basics of folk music while using varying time signatures to entice the listener to expand their listening patterns past learned expectations. I spent many hours at the piano learning music and history through Hungarian folk songs and Bulgarian dance songs. My fingers and my mind were exercised to the fullest.

I stand to greet him and I notice on his notebook he has *Going the Extra Mile* printed on the cover.

He shook my hand and smiled and asked me if I was a pianist. I laughed and said that I was. He said he could tell by the strength and confidence of my handshake.

I asked him who was his greatest inspiration and he said "*It may well be that some composers do not believe in God. All of them, however, believe in Bach.*" That is why we always start our introduction meetings with Bach. He knows how to set a stage and make the rest of us look good. I trust that you have a firm sense of purpose developing over this meeting.

I liked his sense of humour right away. We talked about the importance of going the extra mile and what it truly meant.

Bartok believed that every seed will sprout. He strongly believed that if you render more and better service than you are paid for you will succeed and he then compared it to structure in folk music. He said "*Folk melodies are the embodiment of an artistic perfection of the highest order; in fact, they are models of the way in which a musical idea can be expressed with utmost perfection in terms of brevity of form and simplicity of means.*" In simple terms – keep it simple.

We covered the Law of Increasing Returns and the importance of not holding any resentment, always show concern and courtesy and know that you can not plant seeds on the interstate and think there will be good results. The Law of Compensation knowing everything brings some result, keep things level and fair, and one must have an honest and earnest effort. In a community, you want to be the one that can be called at 2 am. The Law of Contrast and the realization that it is your responsibility to succeed.

From my discussion with Bartok we concluded that it is important to always stay focused on doing your best possible work. To remember that a pleasing attitude is the cornerstone of an attractive personality and that you have to do what needs to be done without being told. Sitting around and waiting for things to happen does not create success. Money is not the only thing that makes you successful. Bartok spent a significant portion of his career studying music from the cultural and social view of those who created it and you could sense the importance of leaving a good stamp in everything that you do.

Bartok closed our session with saying "I cannot conceive of (life or) music that expresses absolutely nothing." Continually challenge yourself. Make your work with joy rather than burden. And remember that peace of mind comes from humility of your own heart. You are amazing soil for seeds to grow brilliantly. Give gratitude everyday.

I sat in my seat and was not able to move. My mind was racing with a sense of creativity that I had never felt before in my life. I had gathered my Big Four and I had asked them to share with me their wisdom and experiences and I received gifts in return that are above measure.

What did I learn from this power session?

Music is a performance. Life is a performance. Sales are a performance. And we all sell in one form or another.

I had met with four different unique personalities and each taught me how to adapt my sense and style to my audience. If I am to be successful with my audience whether it is on a stage, in front of clients, in front of my staff or even working in my community as a volunteer, I have to know my audience and I have to use my definiteness of purpose, my mastermind alliance, my faith and the principle of going the extra mile to succeed.

One major lesson I learned after my meeting was the need to over come fear. So many of use get "*stage fright*" and allow that fright to limit our potential. Not only personally but also professionally.

Overcoming fear was essential in success. Napoleon Hill discussed the seven fears: poverty, criticism, ill health, loss of love, old age, loss of liberty and death.

I would like to encourage each of you to replace fear with hope. Use the firm foundation of Bach to keep you stable, use the charisma of Beethoven to develop your leadership skills, use the faith of Brahms to stir your creative spirit and use Bartok's simplicity of going the extra mile to get you to the next mile. The need to combine faith and a positive mental attitude is essential is all areas of your life.

1. Adopt a definite major purpose.
2. Affirm the object of your desire through prayer.
3. Associate as many as possible of the ten basic human motives.
4. Write out a list of all the advantages of your definite major purpose.
5. Associate with people who are in sympathy with you and your definite major purpose.
6. Do not let one day pass without making at least one move towards your definite major purpose.
7. Choose a pacesetter.
8. Surround yourself with books, pictures, mottoes and other suggestive devices.
9. Never run away from disagreeable circumstances.

10. Anything worth having has a definite piece tag.

As I entered the elevator I hit the main floor button and noticed tiled into the floor were the words *Positive Mental Attitude*. My attitude at the moment was gushing with positivity. Then much to my surprise I noticed behind me in the elevator was Napoleon Hill.

I always enjoy running into Napoleon. I quickly started telling him about how brilliant my meeting with the Big Four went and the many lessons I was going to put into place with my daily life. My daily practise schedule was going to continue to growth with seeds planted in quality soil.

I remember rattling off various examples and finishing with saying that I just could not believe the potential that I had in front of me. Hill put his hand on my shoulder and said "*Whatever the mind can conceive and believe, the mind can achieve*."

**All quotes that are linked in the discussion are actually quotes from Bach, Beethoven, Brahms, Bartok and Hill that have been inserted in the sentence for conversationally development.*

Cynthia (Cyndi) Vos | Bio

Cynthia (Cyndi) Vos, BMus, MEd

Wife. Mother. Entrepreneur. CEO. Business Coach.

Musician. Athlete. Best Selling Author.

Cyndi holds a BMus, Master of Education, Post Graduate Certification in Executive Coaching and she is now completing her final step in Leadership Certification through the Napoleon Hill Foundation.

Cyndi graduated with distinction in her Bachelor degree and then became the youngest student to be accepted into the Masters program, which lead her to a scholarship, which provided the opportunity to study at a Master level in Russia.

Her professional business career began under the direction of her entrepreneurial parents who were followers of the Success Principles. Cyndi focused in healthcare with the company We Care Health Services, specializing in palliative care, for 20 years, serving as the CEO for 10 years. She sold the company when she was 39 and soon to follow the opportunity came to head the final company under the family umbrella with her husband Dave. Cyndi has received many awards for innovation in business including recognition as the Young Entrepreneur of the Year through the Canadian Chamber of Commerce and marketing awards for her philanthropic contributions.

Cyndi has had the opportunity to perform as a solo concert pianist in Canada, England, Poland, Russia, Belarus, Ukraine and the United States.

She is also very active in the fitness community and competes at a national level.

Cyndi can be contacted at cyndibester@gmail.com or follow her at Cyndi Vos on Facebook.

This marks the fourth book that Cyndi has been a contributing author. The first was titled "*The Fine Art of Parenting After Separation: The Power of a Positive Mental Attitude*," the second was "*The Girl in the Red Bikini*" and the third "*Johnny B.*"

CHAPTER 5

The Eight MOST Important SALES Success Strategies

By Mark D. Gleason

The How To and How Not To's

Introduction:

Just about everyone who has ever sold anything has run into objections. Without them, there's usually no sale. With them, there's always the possibility of a sale. And if you get comfortable handling objections, there are potentially many more sales.

For years, sales professionals have attempted to teach sales people how to overcome objections. Here is the thing about handling objections properly: Never give someone the wrong answer if you don't know the right one. Instead, prepare a day ahead of time, if possible, and have the correct response on the tip of your tongue.

This book is about sales success and how to get the most out of your life by selling the most during your life. Sure, there will be obstacles, disappointment, and sadly, there will be many more no's than yes's. But if you follow our eight most important sales success strategies, we are confident that you can become better because you will be armed with a much more organized plan for success. The feeling that we are hoping to have you searching for is that feeling of happiness and pleasure by following each one of our eight sales success strategies. If you are in sales and need a boost to overcome failure, defeat, frustration, and problems, this book is for you. Using our eight sales success strategies will help you cope with the inconsistencies of life. We strongly suggest you stay ambitious and examine all of the options out there. Get yourself aligned properly, and be specific about what your mission in life is. We can't help but be transparent about this fact, there will be surprises, but your progress is dependent on you staying focused and keeping distractions away. We hope you can stay engaged and keep everyone you work with involved, but whatever happens to you, never stop moving and never give up.

Sure, there will be times where you must adjust and accept life's losses and learn from their lessons.

As long as you understand that using our eight sales success strategies to help you analyze and design your next task will eliminate as much of the negatives out of your life. Here is the one question that can transform your sales success strategies: To grow your business beyond anything you've ever imagined, how can I get better?

This book is designed to help you open up to our research and apply it to literally every circumstance. Our eight steps are simple, yet practical, and they have a process associated with them that are all designed to bring your business to a higher plateau.

Sales is not for everyone. But since you got your hands on this material, something really special is in store for you. Sale success is right there waiting for you, but you must reach for it, because it rarely reaches for you. It's imperative that you do the tough things and that you think you can succeed in sales.

We know you will win!

Credits:

Thank you to all of our customers and clients, friends and family. Thank you to our children and grandchildren who have stood by and cheered us on and supported us. Thank you to my wife. Without her, this and our other books wouldn't have been possible.

Sales Success is clearly not for everyone—that's the truth about sales success. But, if you want success in sales more than anything in life, more than life itself, more than most all other areas of your life Then it's time for you to do it or ditch it. Sales success boils down to about four key principles.

First, are you prepared for what's going to be required of you and from you? Sales success becomes a life-changing part of you! So, is it for you?

Second, are your habits (good or bad), aligned with what it will take to make you a sales success? If it's for you, if you are up to it, then let's move onto the third principle of sales success.

The third principle of sales success is the principle of proper planning. Do you, "*the sales professional*," have a written sales success plan? This third principle is simple, but so few sales people actually have a written success plan. Why? There are a number of reasons why sales people don't properly prepare and don't have proper habits. And it shows as a result of their missing written success plans. When you lack basic preparedness, your habits are not congruent with your success plan, or lack thereof. (A PLAN) And you aren't structured properly the fourth key principle, which is THE ACTION PHASE of a sales success plan.

Maybe sales are not for everyone.

Maybe it's not for you? Maybe you didn't know what to do. Do you have the drive? The drive to succeed at all costs. Are you willing to step outside your current comfort zone? Do you have the guts to look inside yourself? Do your behaviors force you to try something new?

Today is the last day to change your ways! Today is the "*best*" day to get out of your own way and start everything over in a new way. The most effective ways to become a sales success is to change your techniques and find new, effective ways to achieve sales success. Remember, nothing great is easy, and nothing easy is great.

Are you willing to live up to your potential? There's a good chance that Sales Success isn't for you?

Our experience training, coaching, and mentoring over a thousand sales people over nearly four decades has revealed some eye-opening facts. Approximately 90-95% of the so-called "*salespeople*" aren't willing to pay the price. Why? It mostly boils down to a lack of commitment. In fact, this "paying the price" principle is one of the eight big sales success principles you must address and face if you're going to make it into the lofty 5% of the best sales professionals on the planet. The majority of sales people limit themselves by a lack of commitment to themselves. The majority of salespeople just aren't willing to do what it will take, and they won't show up when it's most important. It appears the unsuccessful look for the short cut, the easy way, the quick fix. All of those qualities are nothing but excuses to avoid the hard work it's going to take to be a sales success.

Our Eight Sales Success principles

You must ask yourself about these every day. These eight principles are strategies that are non-negotiable.

Let us welcome you into our wonderful world of sales success. It's not easy, so stop what you're doing and start doing something totally different. Let's get you started on the road to amazing life changes.

"*Nothing changes until you change*."

The Eight Principles to Sales Success

1. Has today been filled with positive, encouraging thoughts?
2. Has anyone influenced me today positively or negatively?
3. Have I taken the training and applied it?
4. Am I working hard or hardly working?
5. Do I realize that success is not obtained overnight?
6. Have I organized my day and know the value of my time $5 - $500 - $5,000?
7. Am I willing to commit and control my emotions?
8. Am I willing to pay the price?

Let's start from the top and dissect principle #1.

Principle #1

It's all about staying positive during our 57,000 daily conversations that we have with ourselves. Are you filling your mind with upbeat, encouraging ideas? Do you spend your time with positive people who support you? Is there more things going right with you than wrong with you? You may not even see what others see about you. But are you attracting other positive, upbeat relationships? Or, are you dragging down your friends and associates?

The negative side of some people is so repellent that they're their own worst enemy. They seem to spew negative nonsense, and no one wants to hear it or associate with it. They have a problem for every solution. Negative people stand smack dab in the way of their own sales success, and most don't even recognize it. And the result of it is impossible to mask. Their sales numbers never lie! It's always bad about the other guy. The problem with negative people is that they forget that it's always about the client and never about you or your experiences.

That's the magic formula of the most successful sales professionals. Those who have a limited time to spend and they choose wisely to focus and speak about the other guy, and next to nothing about what they think, or about how great they are.

That's the power of principle #1—it's a positive way to keep other people's attention. YOU focus on their positive points of interest. (People hate to be sold, but oh man, do they love to buy.) The upbeat, superstar sales professionals have made staying positive their way of life, helping people buy. They sell it by speaking positively about the lives of their consumers. They don't need to work at it, it just comes naturally.

Do you?

Have you personally audio or videotaped your last few customer interactions? If you have, you'd probably wished you would have invested in Pepto-Bismol stock from a serious dose of upset stomach-it is. Here is what you will have heard, too much speaking, and it's almost always about yourself. Simple fix, shut up and listen to the consumer. Biggest news flash most sales people miss out on is this. They can't help talking about their favorite subject: themselves. Here is a super success sales secret: "*Speak no more about you forever more*." If you catch yourself talking about yourself, make sure it's a positive not a negative. Nothing turns off the water spigot of sales like a negative comment.

After four decades in sales at the highest level, there are few principles or strategies that separate the average from the superstars more than a positive, optimistic outlook. Nothing will kill a sale quicker than a negative comment, or worse yet, a sales person who moans on about themselves and their life.

Ask yourself this question, it's the #1 question, and it's from the #1 success principle: Has today been filled with positive encouraging thoughts?

If your answer wasn't, "*yes, today's been a positive day*," then you need to reevaluate the way you're going through your day. You are as positive as you make up your mind to be. Being upbeat and positive is a choice. The same goes for negativity—it's a choice. Here's a great question: if you had to invest your life savings with someone, would you prefer a positive person or the negative one? You'd probably choose a positive over the negative person about every time. It's not that tricky. It's a pretty easy question to answer, isn't it? Most everyone wants to work with the optimist. Are you any different? Probably not, in fact, people report being excited to make a decision when they're being counseled by an optimistic person.

Which is why the second principle to sales success is so important.

Principle #2

Has anyone influenced me today positively or negatively?

That's the direct result from the super successful sales professionals, of which those who are positive have the most success. They influence the consumers to make a decision, being positive creates the most natural form of urgency. It's like a smile, or a hug of reassurance. But the effect on a sales decision by being negative usually leads a buyer's decision in the opposite direction. Negative influences and attitudes get many more "*no*" responses than "*yes*" responses ever get. A negative way of thinking affects everyone. It's called "*Life's Biggest Turn-off*."

What way do you sell and how does your attitude affect people?

Are you in the top 5-10% of the salespeople in your organization?

Do you have a positive or negative sales approach?

Ask yourself these questions every day.

If you're going to get to the top of your sales field, your sales success will be directly tied to how you're being affected either positively or negatively by the people around you every day. Make sure you find the good in everything you do, and let people know about the positives you see in them, too.

This is our best-suggested training and it's about all we can recommend.

Which is why sale success principle #3 is so important.

Principle #3

Have you taken the training and applied it?

Successful sales professionals never stop learning; they are seminar junkies. They get hooked on continuing education. They never quit—they always work on their scripts and dialogues. They take the training and teach themselves, then they apply it into the action phase of their plans. You can see them go, and go, and go, as they grow, and grow, and grow. For them, continuing education is non-negotiable. For instance, one super successful sales associate practiced 10 times for that one opportunity moment to shine. The successful sales professional sees ongoing training as the only way to properly prepare.

That's the deal the super successful make with themselves—they work harder on themselves than they do on anything else they do.

So another question you must ask yourself everyday and it is a big one...

Strategy #4

Are you working hard or hardly working?

This is one of the most important action steps in every aspect of a sales success business plan. So are you working hard or hardly working? One person said, "*Whatever you're doing, you'd better do more if you're going to be doing more*." The majority of sales people think they're busy when all they do is run a few errands, return a few emails, check in with social media, and plan lunch. They call this their business plan. It's really a busy-ness plan that's not really all that busy. Why is that? Probably because they're unwilling to do whatever it takes to be a sales success. What it says loud and clear is, "*they're soon to be out of here*." We've discovered that this principle of hardly working is at the root of most of the unsuccessful sales people. They think they're working hard, but that's their excuse to remain the same. But none of the super successful sales professionals ever remain the same. The superstars are always finding ways to work smarter and work harder.

Are you? Are you working hard? Could you get up one hour earlier every day? If you got to work one hour earlier every day and you completely applied yourself during that one-hour, it would have the effect of adding 2.5 weeks of productivity to your year. And that is working smarter. So rise earlier, work smarter, earn more! Pretty simple advice, right? But, are you looking the "*quick fix?*" Are you searching for the "*shortcuts?*" If so, you're only fooling yourself, there are no shortcuts or quick fixes. The only way to do anything is the right way, which is hard work.

Don't get stressed out, just do the hard work and realize, it'll take time, which is why sales success principle #5 is so important.

Principle #5

Do you realize that success is not obtained overnight?

Everyone hopes for the "*Lotto Lifestyle*"—becoming an overnight success. But success rarely happens overnight, and rarely does a "*Lotto Lifestyle*" way of thinking ever work.

All great things take time to work out and it's important to remember that. No one becomes an overnight sales success. It takes time, patience, persistence, and personal growth. Obtaining sales success is a process, and you must believe in yourself more than anyone else believes in you. Are you willing to do the hard work, and are you willing to keep doing the hard work? I If you're not, you're destined to remain the same and will find yourself in the 90% group—the group of average sales people. Maybe you don't know what you're truly worth. Maybe you're willing to settle. Maybe you have got no idea what your time per hour is truly worth.

This is why Principle #6 is so important for your growth potential. When was the last time you analyzed what you earn per hour? This might scare you into action, or it might drive you out of sales into a more dollar-productive, hourly wage occupation.

Either way, figuring out your dollar-per-hour value is the only sales success plan that will sober you up.

Principle #6

Do you know the value of your time? Can you literally put a dollar value per hour on it?

If you're not sure, it's time you figure it out and decide what's the best way to move forward with your future life in sales.... Or if it's best not to.

Let's start by taking the average of your last ten commissions, and divide the number of hours into the dollars to arrive at your dollar-per-hour value. Is it as high as you'd hoped? You have to be realistic, yet serious about your earning goals. Many companies pays $10-$15 per hour, guaranteed, for the exact number of hours you put in. Also consider there are little to no additional costs associated with being one of someone else's employee.

Part of our time value equation evaluation involves a personal assessment of our 96 15-minute daily intervals. Start by making a list of what you are doing every 15 minutes for an entire day, then categorize that list by putting together items that you are spending most of your time doing. Once you're done with that, remove one item per day from your current daily routine list that you identify as a time-waster or a non-money-maker, until you discover which one item pays you the most. Take that one item and devote yourself to that one item. Now separate this from the really important matters that should be taking up approximately 50% of your time, (God, spouse, family, etc.) as these are non-negotiable time items. The remaining 50% of your time should go to that one item that makes you the most money. After all, if the number one item creates 50-60% of your income, then it deserves 50-60% of your focus.

What we've uncovered is that most salespeople don't know how much per hour they're earning. Why? Maybe they don't want to know, or they're embarrassed. Before too much more time goes by, wouldn't it be in your best interests to know?

We can assure you this: the top-of-the-line, super successful sales professionals know what their time is worth and they waste very little of it on matters that don't matter. These same individuals avoid interruptions at all costs, they improve themselves daily, apply the training, and prove it every second, and that's why they commit to everything they do.

This is a list of what $5/hour salespeople might be doing:

*Small tasks
*Delivery
*Tiny purchases
*Discussions with unqualified prospects
*Website analysis
*Cleaning up
*Basic follow-up
*Over-meeting mania
*Minimum wage
*Simple solutions
*Email miniscule
*Simplified outsourcing

This is a list of what $500/hour salespeople might be doing:

*Discussions with qualified prospects

*Prioritizing time management of personal processes

*Sales lead generation (prospecting)

*Negotiating above-average deals

*Social media, if done well

*Complex task assignment(s)

This is a list of what $5,000/hour salespeople might be doing:

*Writing super sales copy

*Manage money properly

*Execute cutting edge and implementation

*Quality writing time

*Negotiating major league deals

*Higher end clientele

*Getting proper teammates on board

*Delegation of multi-levels and streams of income

*Closing top line transactions

*Speaking publicly

This brings us to the important Principle #7.

Strategy #7

Are you really willing to commit to improve you and everything you do?

Here is where the proverbial rubber meets the road. Most everyone can easily say, "*I'll commit*," but then life gets in the way. Something more important comes up and we avoid holding ourselves accountable to any other commitments we have made. We call these excuses or gross rationalizations. These are how we explain away to ourselves, how and why we didn't finish what we started. Excuses are also used to justify why we delay starting something and it's ultimately why we back down from a commitment. So many people's good intentions to do something, complete a chore, make that call or get back up after having been knocked down. Are you one of those unwilling to dance through the fire? Are you going to go about your way quietly, ending up ashamed of your own lack of follow-through? We can assure you this—and you've probably guess it by now—sales success superstars honor their commitments. They live up to the responsibilities that come as a result of having committed to themselves.

They're the ones who're willing to face the consequences of having failed, but continue to follow through.

They commit to what it takes to start and to finish a big project, sale, or task. There are NO excuses, period. The committed don't get up to fail, they just never fail to get up!

They go about doing the extra, beyond where they thought they'd go; they go the extra mile. Their commitments have become their cornerstone of behaviors. They don't refuse to do what's necessary, they do what's needed.

They make a bold commitment and stand by it. This is the reason why doors open—they put their hearts into everything they do. They shine because they commit, that's why the work they do matters. They're unwilling to leave any of it until later. It's what the successful people do, they show what they're worth because of their work. Committing to do what's needed to do.

That's why they do it…

Sales success is about making a commitment and truly sticking to it. Is that what you do?

However, a super successful salesperson comes around full circle, which brings us to our final strategy.

Strategy #8

Are you willing to pay the price?

This is a huge question, and the truth is that for the vast majority of salespeople, the answer is "No." Most salespeople think that their results speak for themselves. They decided consciously or unconsciously that they were willing to accept their own productive or unproductive results. We simply call it their sales numbers. Sales statistics are inescapable results.

Are you willing to do what it will take to "make it" as a super sales success? Only you can answer this question, but a year from now if you measure how far you've come in that year and you're not satisfied, you've got a chance to improve. The cost you must pay to be a sales superstar isn't cheap, easy, or quick. It's hard and it's going to take a lot more training. Success will involve reading everything you can get your hands and listening to everything you can get your ears on.

Here's a suggestion: surround yourself with more successful people and you'll soon be more successful. As your income will be the average of the five closes associates average incomes. As the old adage states, "*You will become just like who you will be associating with.*" Be patient; it takes time to realize that it takes time to improve yourself. Do you realize it yet – that if today's not another positive day, you had better do something to make it a better day.

Here's the challenge for most people. You have to do more to become more and that takes being positive more often. The effect of being positive more often- will have a positive effect on more people.

Some additional suggestions: never quit working hard and never leave something you can do today until tomorrow. This is all part of the sales success plan.

If you want more, you've got to become more. Are you going to do everything necessary to be a sales success superstar?

Skipping any of the eight principles to sales success is not suggested. If you're already at the top of your sales game, remember that staying there is harder than getting there. That's why it's so important to reevaluate these eight sales success principles every day. And if you're willing and not scared to go beyond where you currently are, then nothing is impossible.

These success principles are just part of it, but if you want to go even higher. You've got to improve upon your sales questions. Selling is story telling. Selling makes life less boring.

That is why in sales, your income will be in direct proportion to the quality of the questions you ask. This is why it's so important to keep asking yourself these eight great Sales success principle questions every day. Now, how you answer them is going to determine your future destiny.

Are you willing to look yourself in the eye and ask and answer these questions, making a promise to yourself? If you're unwilling to commit, if you're not able to be all you can be, there's nothing left for any of us to do to help you see. Nobody said, "*it will be easy*", no one ever really thinks it'll happen quickly. But if you're willing to start working really hard on your most valuable asset, you – then nothing's impossible.

So let's get started...

What one thing are you going to do every day to change your life in a positive way?

What effect are you going to have on the world every day?

What are you going to implement today to make things happen?

Are you going to get up a little earlier, work harder, and are you going to do things better tomorrow than you did today? Are you going to keep repeating these things every day?

Are you going to avoid interruptions at all costs, as this is the only way you'll realize what your time is truly worth?

Is it reality for you to pay the price from this day forward?

No one has these answers but you. Somethings are meant to be, but we hope that you take ahold of your life's plan and get a grip on all that life has available for you to do. Remember, if it's to be, it's always up to me. No one can do this for you, and no one will do this for you! People will go about as far in life as they make up their minds to go. Do you have a higher calling? Do you have what it takes to be a sales success? What is it you want for your life, and what are you willing to do to get it?

If you want it all, the only question is this: Will I do whatever it takes as long as it takes me to make it?

Here are the four simple how-tos:

1. Prepare properly.
2. Get into the right habits.
3. Have a written success plan.
4. Get into massive action, acting on your plan.

That's how it's got to be, if you're going to be a sales success. You can make anything of yourself that you want too. Again, nothing that is great is easy, and nothing easy is great. And everything great takes time, and it's time that makes the most of everything great.

Every step, every aspect of sales success takes a lifetime of dedication to improve on everything you do. Hold this fact close to your heart because nothing happens just because. It's the same with every sale; each one sale happens because of you and all the little things that you do.

You persist in personal improvement, success systems improvement, and relationship success improvements.

This is all part of it, are you ready, willing, and able?

Are you willing to do what it's going to take to get to the top?

Our hope is that your answer is YES!

But only you can answer that question.

Mark Gleason | Bio

Have you endured the embarrassment and rejection of having failed in sales? Well if you have, Mark can relate to you and with you.

What could be more inspirational then actually selling a home your parents owned and making the sale at the age of ten? Well for Mark Gleason, it was just another chapter in his long and winding "sales life." His earliest attempt at sales however began with his own snake farm, eventually going door-to-door at nine years old attempting to sell his snakes. Mark said selling snakes was all about being optimistic.

Mark's real entrepreneurial career is best known for his role as being a top listing and selling realtor. He has managed and owned multiple business enterprises, real estate developments, and housing projects where all of them are centered on massive sales.

A lifetime of learning and continuous self-improvement is always what brings him back to his personal relationships and the best way to help his clients and customers.

Mark says, "*Never stop learning and always keep testing out what's working and not working.*" He has written 28 books about selling and motivation, and Mark is still at work, selling at the highest levels. Mark has been married to his wife Kim for the past 30 years. They are blessed to have three daughters.

Mark and Kim can be reached at www.soldbygleason.com

CHAPTER 6

AN ATTITUDE OF EXCELLENCE—

By Rudy Kusuma

Building the #1 Real Estate Sales Team

Typical...this is what a majority of real estate agents are. Sure, there are efforts to market and promote yourself as distinct, but in the end, one thing remains consistent for almost every agent out there: they do everything from beginning to end with their transactions, and I mean everything. This includes:

- Communication with clients
- All the details of the transaction
- Negotiating the contracts
- Putting up the For Sale sign

And every one of the other steps that take a buyer or seller to their closing I couldn't tell you how long it's been that way, exactly, but I'd venture to say that it's as close "*to the beginning*" as you could get. Maybe it's time that agents consider putting their days as a one-man operation to an end for everyone's benefit.

I instantly loved real estate when I entered into it, and found a commitment to it that I knew would last me a lifetime. Because of this, I began reflecting on how different people-oriented professions managed their business. It's very seldom that one person wears every hat. Instead, they choose to focus on a specific aspect of the business and become specialized in that area. They have a general knowledge of "*the business*," but specific expertise. When was the last time that anyone went to visit a doctor or lawyer and that individual managed everything by themselves? It just doesn't happen, and I saw that the real estate industry was truly doing itself a disservice by not finding the strengths in people to maximize the potential of a great consumer experience. You see, every detail is important to the "*overall experience*," which is the hub of my business model for the cohesive team that I'm so excited to be a part of.

AT THE HEART OF IT LIES CORE VALUES

The realization that there was a more cohesive and unified way to give people a fantastic real estate experience was brought to light from a most unexpected experience. My family and I went on a Disney cruise. I'm not certain how many of you have ever been on one or had the "*Disney experience*," but it is incredible. Everyone knows their role and is masterful at it, lending to a more amazing experience for the customer. So inspiring!

The feeling that my experience gave me stayed with me and in 2007, when the inspiration to be a part of a team that met this concept came, I already knew that it had to be a "*clients first*" experience. This sounds well enough, of course, and it is something that most every agent in the industry would likely say. I knew that doing it was different. I had to seek out people who had an instinctual understanding that:

Everyone on this team had to be really happy and enjoy what they did.

This was a profound moment for me and it quickly became the focal point of the efforts to build a team that was "the best of the best." Having a core set of values that we all naturally gravitated toward was a criterion that could not be negotiable. Through this, we could create a strong culture that naturally created synergy, transferring a level of excitement we had as a team to our clients' ultimate experience. If Disney could do this with thousands of employees, there was definitely a way to master this with less than twenty-five employees.

Through experiences and growth and constant re-evaluation, the business model that I've come up with consists of eight core values, all which are designed to celebrate a team that really cares about what happens to each other. This is what naturally leads to a "*clients first*" experience.

CORE VALUE #1: DELIVER "*WOW*" THROUGH SERVICE.

When I first got started in the business, I saw that there were two basic types of agents that consumers came into contact with:

- The agent who had no time. They're good agents but too busy, because they are a one-man show.
- The agent who has a lot of time. They have nothing to do and spend a lot of their time cold

calling and knocking on doors, hoping they'll catch a break.

Most clients see these two types of agents and they get mixed emotions. They want the best of both worlds—the successful agent and the agent who has time to make them feel like they are their only client. Why not give clients both worlds?

"*Put your money where your mouth is.*" is a fairly common phrase, and I'm guessing that you've heard it. We take this phrase to heart with our team, because we know that once someone hires an agent they have entered into a contract that is not easily broken. Contracts are a much bigger risk for the client than the agent, typically, which is why we offer a few incentives that help reverse the risk and put the clients at ease. This lends credibility to our determination to provide a "*client first*" experience. The three incentives that have worked particularly well for us affirming the beliefs we have about this experience are:

1. We have a performance guarantee. This states that if their home doesn't sell, we will buy it.
2. If we don't return a telephone call within 24 hours, we'll give you $500.00. Having clients know that they do come first and that we're committed to their experience with our team is imperative to our success, and it's proven to be an award winning formula.
3. Property purchase promise. If you purchase one of our listings and are not happy with that property within the next three years, we'll resell it at no cost to you.

You see, it's not good enough to just take a client from Point A to Point B. Just like on the cruise, at the end of it, you want the clients saying, "*Wow! This is great and I don't want it to end.*" In real estate terms, this translates into us not wanting the clients to feel that our journey is done just because they've closed on their home. This is important because the measurement of success really comes in the clients' reviews, testimonials, and if they refer other people to us. And that is why we bring the "*WOW*" to service and we don't settle for just closing the deal.

CORE VALUE #2: EMBRACE CHANGE

In real estate, being stuck in a certain way will assure you of one thing—that you are going to be stuck for a long time, growing stagnant, and eventually making your relevancy in your market go extinct. There is a choice to not allow this to happen, which is why our team:

- Embraces technology, knowing that it can help us serve our clients better, and even improve how well we can do our specialties within the team.
- Gives a concerted effort to stay on top of laws and regulations, which always change on a daily basis.

We always make sure that our clients get the latest and best technology, the best experience, the best '*whatever*' change the industry has. We are not staying constant. One of the best ways we've been able to create this noticeable distinction in our market is by utilizing the "*talking house.*" This is a program where someone can tune into a radio station that, while driving by a property listed for sale, would give sale information for the driver to hear all about it.

Capturing potential buyers during a moment of excitement is a strong strategy, and it would be hard to capitalize on that with an actual person, as instantaneous availability is rare. Technology is a wonderful companion to the real estate industry.

CORE VALUE #3: PURSUE GROWTH

Our team is comprised of 26 team members at this time. Something that others will frequently hear me mention is, "*It seems like we are a real estate company, but in reality, at the core of it, we are a personal growth development company. We just use real estate as a vehicle to do that.*" It's an interesting statement, one which often draws attention. This is what it means:

> *Every morning we spend one hour doing training. On Saturday mornings, we hold personal goals meeting, where we dive into our mastermind and discuss books that will help us grow as individuals and within the team environment. One example of a book that we've gone through is Jack Canfield's Success Principles.*

What we wish to achieve is about more than getting leads and referrals, it's about ensuring that we grow as individuals. That is how you make a team stronger and experience how it starts to shine, or shine brighter in this case.

CORE VALUE #4: HAVE FUN

We all enjoy what we do, which makes for such a fun

work environment. This type of infectious nature carries over into what clients feel when they walk into our office. They don't need to hear us say we are a team—they feel how we are a team.

It's all about keeping it fun and interesting, as well. For example, at least once a month—most often the last Friday of the month—we have what's called a "*performance club*." This club is for everybody who receives at least one endorsement and referral from clients. We do something fun to celebrate this. In the past, we've gone to Las Vegas, went shooting, to Disneyland, or go a bit smaller— hanging out at the bar and having a great meal. The purpose is to celebrate, because these individual accolades are all a part of making a stronger team.

CORE VALUE #5: OPEN COMMUNICATION

Since we run our operation as a team, the clients only have one point of contact for each part of their transaction. In order to keep this flow and process running smoothly, we need to have open internal communication to have maximum effectiveness with our client communication. To do this, we:

- Make sure that clients always know what stage of their transaction they are at and everything involving it.
- Use our daily hour meeting to address anything that may impact our operations, remaining mindful to our ultimate goals as a team.
- Operate as a "*flat organization*." There is no hierarchy or bureaucracy, because we don't want to focus on office politics; only what is best for the client.

Communication is an art form and together, we've found a way to ensure that we are paying attention to how we do it and always remembering why it's so important!

CORE VALUE #6: POSITIVE TEAM SPIRIT

Every person who enters our office notices a few things immediately.

- **First**, we have no walls,, which means no private offices. Closed off spaces leads to a team that's not as cohesive as it could be.
- **Second**, when people walk into our office—clients especially—they are greeted with people looking at them, smiling, and showing that they are welcome, not an intrusion. It's genuine!

These steps, while unheard of in many real estate environments, are one of our strongest attributing factors for our success. There's a sense of joy, and people reveal how appealing this is through their expressions toward us.

CORE VALUE #7: BE PASSIONATE

Our team is about more than selling homes. From within, we truly are a personal growth company. Achieving personal and professional excellence is our mission and that's the type of people we attract to the team. Our passion is enthusiastic and we realize the purpose in everything that we do, each and every day.

Every Tuesday we hold various seminars in our office, inviting people from the community in. We are consistent and deliver great information and people know this—making it a ten-plus-year tradition. We deliver without fail and we're consistent, not growing tired of the knowledge we have to share, because we are all so passionate about it.

The people that become a part of our team have this clear understanding of the qualities that are expected from them. For some, it may be a bit too much, and that's okay. We are not for everyone— we are for those who want to find genuine satisfaction and fulfillment through using our business model—the "*client first*" formula.

CORE VALUE #8: GIVING BACK TO THE COMMUNITY

For every transaction our team does, a portion of the income goes to the children's hospital in our area. For one example, this year we are on a mission to raise $100,000. Our team wants to be a part of our community, not just a stellar sales team, and giving back exemplifies how important this is to us. It's more than words; it's actions. So, where some people will give a client a gift card, maybe, to show their appreciation, we can think of no better gift for us to give our clients or community than the gift of giving back to the community as a whole. Stronger communities make for happier residents within them, and this inspires us.

Never losing sight of where we can go…

Our desire to have a client-centric real estate team structure based on a proactive sales system that serves our VIP clients—which is every client—with less hassle, is what we are always working toward. It motivates all of us and keeps us on track.

At this time, we're not quite there, but we are the #1 team for ReMax Systems in California. We have our sights set on becoming the #1 team in the United States this year, and from there, we hope that it will continue to grow. And as it does, I'm excited to see how this business model and team that we've created is cultivating leaders to make other teams that have the same core values. Basically, through our commitment and showing the rewards of a "*client first*" approach, we are revamping the perception of real estate agents for consumers everywhere—and this is an exciting change!

Rudy L. Kusuma | Bio

Rudy L. Kusuma is an investor, best-selling author, business coach, entrepreneur, and top-producing real estate agent. He is the Founder and CEO of RE/MAX TITANIUM and the Managing Director of TEAM NUVISION, the #1 Real Estate Sales Team in San Gabriel Valley. He has been recognized as one of the Top 100 team leaders in RE/MAX Worldwide (out of 100,000 real estate agents).

Rudy and his team have sold over $500 Million in transactions. He has been awarded multiple top producers awards, including The Five Star Real Estate Professional Award as published in the Los Angeles Magazine, and named as one of America's Best Real Estate Agents as published in The Wall Street Journal.

As a philanthropist, Rudy is on a mission to raise $100,000 for the Children's Hospital in downtown Los

Angeles. For every house that his team sells, Rudy and his team are donating a portion of their income to the Children's Hospital. Not only home sellers benefit from his team's award-winning service, but they donate a substantial portion of their income on every home sale to help the local children in the community.

Rudy has advised and counseled homebuyers, sellers, and real estate investors from every walk of life. CEO's, executives, and business owners hire his team because their businesses are "*Teams*", so they understand and appreciate Rudy's Team Home Selling System. Sales Professionals and Marketing-Oriented Entrepreneurs hire Rudy's team because they quickly recognize the superiority of Rudy's sophisticated System for selling homes as quickly as possible, for top dollars. Doctors, Hospital Administrators, and Nurses hire Rudy's team because, like the executives, they are thoroughly familiar with the benefits of a Team Approach. Exceptionally busy couples hire Rudy's team because his home selling system features methods of marketing and selling homes that minimizes their involvement and inconvenience.

Rudy provides numerous public resources regarding how to buy and sell real estate in today's real estate market. In addition, as a Certified Distressed Property Expert, Rudy contributes weekly articles on foreclosure prevention options available to homeowners. His expert advice has been published by community newspapers, including: Indonesia Media, Mid Valley News, Temple City Life, Temple City Tribune, Arcadia Weekly, Monrovia Weekly, El Monte Examiner, San Gabriel Sun, Duarte Dispatch, Rosemead Reader, Azusa Beacon, and Around Alhambra.

Rudy L. Kusuma is the author of The Ultimate NO HOLDS BARRED Guide to Selling & Buying a Home in the

San Gabriel Valley and the co-author of the book that will change the landscape of real estate industry, Death of the Traditional Real Estate Salesperson: Rise of The Super-Profitable Real Estate Sales Team.

Rudy L. Kusuma lives in Temple City with his wife and two sons. He can be reached online at: www.TeamNuVision.net or by telephone at 626-780-2221.

CHAPTER 7

Success in Real Estate Requires One Primary Super Power: Giving to Others

By Nancy Alert

*"When one person gives,
two people receive."*

"Hello! I am Nancy Alert. I get it done!"

It is important to understand that the biggest challenge with which you will deal with in sales is not the competition. That is the least of your worries. The biggest hurdle you must overcome instead is what goes on in your head...the thoughts you think and the energy you put out into the world. I ran across that sentiment the other day. It made perfect sense. However, I wish I would have been introduced to such an idea 20 years ago. But, I guess that's okay. I have had a wonderful career within the real estate industry and have no regrets. Yes, I have traveled a path with numerous stumbling blocks thrown in front of me. What has continually set me apart from the rest of the pack, though, is my innate ability – and unwavering confidence – to turn them over into stepping-stones.

But let me assure you…I wasn't always this confident.

It's quite amusing to me now that some people with whom I associate jokingly (and lovingly, too!) refer to me as Nancy "*Assert*." I suppose assertiveness is a hallmark of my personality at this point in my life. However, during my professional formative years, I was anything but. If I even opened my mouth back then, it was probably to yawn or take a bite of food….but to speak my mind and enjoy the results? I never could have imagined! It is possible to realize phenomenal success strictly on commission, but you do have to put in the sweat equity.

For the past two decades, I have been a professional real estate agent living on 100% commission. That is a mighty statement right there. It has been either feast of famine at times; chicken or feathers. There were periods of time when I wasn't even certain if I could put food on my table. While I could not control the external factors in the world contributing to the down times, I could control my attitude towards them, and that positive attitude has continually shaped my entire life, courtesy of the journey I pursued every day.

I was born in Guyana, South America and was raised in Brooklyn, New York. When it was time for me to attend college, there was only one university on my radar: Howard University in Washington, DC. Ever since I was a young girl, I sensed that was where I needed to embrace my academic aspirations. I earned my degrees in Environmental Science & Design and in Marketing. I have always been an ambitious individual.

After graduation, I immediately transitioned to an internship specializing in management. Needless to say, it didn't take long for me to realize this was not the place for me. Getting up at six in the morning every day was not something for which I was built. I mean, rising at the crack of dawn? Who does that? I am far more productive later in the day and into the evening hours. I am also not a cubicle kind of gal and am definitely not cut out to repot to a boss other than myself. I began to ask myself, "*What can I do for money that allows me to meet people (something I enjoy!) and help them along the way?*"

As I was speaking with a friend about my quandary at the time, she suggested I look into real estate. She had given it a try but only lasted a couple of months, so one might wonder why I would even take advice from her. But, as she began to describe the professional environment of this industry, I realized that it might be a great fit for me. After passing a few hurdles, such as studying for the real estate exam and passing it, I began my career in 1996 and haven't looked back since.

It would be quite easy for me to say I've had a stellar career. After all, if I had a Hall of Fame in my name, it would showcase a few show-stopping awards, including my nomination into the RE/MAX Hall of Fame for earning over a million dollars in two years; being showcased in Who's Who in Black Washington, DC and featured as a technology innovator in Black Enterprise Magazine. While I am certainly proud of my accomplishments, those are merely by-products of hard work and determination in my desire to not only successfully close a deal, but to also open new relationships. To make it in the real estate industry, the driving force comes in the form of relationships.

"I literally have no idea what I am doing!"

—(Just a bit about my
background!)

When I first began treading the real estate waters, I had to quickly learn to navigate this new terrain. Fortunately, I worked with a team of agents who took the time to answer my questions and help me. There was not this sense of competition as you might think. Yes, you are competing with each other to some degree, but overall, the road to success should always be paved with acts of kindness, encouragement and helpfulness towards those with whom you work.

As a result of the mentors early on in my career who took the time and interest in answering all of my questions and lighting my path, I have since become that esoteric fountain of knowledge for those who are now learning from me. And I love it! I will answer questions and inquiries of all types, not just those related to real estate, and I have never been known to go halfway with a response. If you ask me a question, I will jump in and provide a full report in return. No one ever gets cheated when it comes to gathering information from me. Further, if I don't know the answer, I will research it until I do. Giving 100% is more than a baseline effort for me; it's just a starting point.

When I first began my career in real estate back in 1996 (when the market was down I definitely had some courage!), I started at the Weichart office in Annandale Virginia. I was just 28 years old and the youngest in the group. Most of them were in their 40s, 50s, and 60s. I was still wet behind the ears yet very eager to learn and soak up their knowledge and wisdom. I have no shame reflex in admitting that I had absolutely no idea what I was doing, but I translated that fear to courage. Fortunately, the team at Weichart was quite helpful. I took a cue from their willingness to help me and have since translated that attitude towards those coming into the industry on my heels. Today, I routinely have agents from other companies and around the country even calling me to ask me questions. Sure, they could inquire of their brokers, but they come to me because I take the time to listen and respond. If someone asks me a question, I make sure to have an answer. I absorb knowledge from a variety of sources: books, seminars, videos and more. I never stop the learning process. I am not and have never desired to be a cookie cutter realtor. I have a creative edge that lends itself well towards making things happen. If there is ever a challenge or an obstacle, I can develop a solution. That is what my clients like about me, as I am always "*getting it done.*"

After leaving Weichart in 2005, I transitioned to RE/MAX Allegiance, which was a great time as the market was on fire! I loved every minute of it. After polishing my skills there for 10 years, I then relocated to Keller Williams and am now with Better Homes & Gardens Real Estate. Yes, I have made some significant changes throughout my career, but change is good. I just knew instinctively when to switch gears, and with every change, new experiences, challenges and rewards appeared. Growth is definitely a great learning tool.

Nancy Alert, The Early Years: Does she even speak?

After I graduated from Howard University, I was ready to hit the ground running. I made sure that by the time I graduated, I did not owe any money in terms of student loan debt. I was successfully able to fund my academic career through myriad scholarships and grants. Getting through college was totally up to me. My parents did not have the financial resources to assist me, so I was completely on my own in this regard. Looking back, this was important training for my lean years within the real estate arena, as it taught me how to budget and live on limited sources of income when required. It also helped to shape my resolve to make it through any challenge.

When I was ready to cross the threshold from the halls of academia to actually earning a real pay check as a bona fide professional, I relied on a paid internship I had started while actually in my undergraduate studies. This particular internship transitioned me to a management job after college. As a result of that endeavor, I was able to purchase a new car and my first condominium. I was the epitome of success in my opinion!

By age 28, I was married (I checked this off the list), and that same year I began my illustrious career as a Realtor. I did all the things you were "*supposed*" to do in my 20s: I got a car; I got insurance; I started a savings account; I got a job; and I even participated in some stock trading on my own. I relied heavily on my penchant for self-discovery and learning. I love to educate myself and would always read...a lot! I still do! I can talk a little bit about many things. I suppose you could say I am a mile wide and an inch deep! I love to learn, even if it's only a little bit about something, but learning opens so many doors for you, and it is always great to somehow remain a part of the conversation...any conversation! Besides, because I was so shy when I was younger, I wanted to have the confidence a wealth of information provides you. I wanted to walk into a room and be able to navigate most any dialogue or conversation with ease. I desired to speak to someone on any level about anything or any topic and appear confident and aware of the subject matter at hand. To this day, I devour information voraciously, as it fuels myself and enhances my networking abilities. This former wallflower is never at a loss for words now!

The 10 Keys to Real Estate Success

In my book of real estate success, this would have to be the shortest chapter. The first key to success in real estate is to call me. From there, I will handle the other nine! If you want something, you call Nancy Alert. In order to secure success in this industry, you have to be a problem solver and have a nose for solutions. That is what clients want and deserve. And for the record, I have never met a problem I couldn't solve! Creativity is key sometimes. If a client does not have the money to facilitate the transaction, I will go find the money. As a creative Real Estate Broker, I help clients find funding for development projects, financing multi-million dollar deals through private or hard money financing. If a client discovers a tax lien upon the property or cannot secure a loan due to bad credit, I will turn that potentially negative situation into a positive one. I am not the cookie cutter Realtor who simply fills in the blanks and completes the forms. I allow my creative instincts to go to work and make each transaction a successful and enjoyable one. If a client wants something, they know to call me. As I always like to say, I get things done!

Don't be afraid to open your mouth and say something!

When I was young and crossing the threshold into this new career for me, I was extremely shy, and painfully so. That statement bears repeating, as it could have held me back if I allowed it to do so. You could barely get me to say too words at the time. I was really good at knowing what type of footwear people wore, as my eyes were usually fixated towards the ground. I would have much rather sat on the sidelines than to participate in the game. I honestly could not look someone in the eye when I was talking to them...probably because I was barely speaking, anyway! Real estate is what opened the door for me...and is what helped me to open my mouth and speak up. I realized that if I did not learn to exercise more confidence, I would starve. I had to eat to survive, and the only way I could put food on my table was to overcome my shyness. Was it easy? Not at all, but I had to force myself out of my comfort zone to find my way to the path of success.

But it is more than just talking to people. Once you gain the confidence to speak up and speak out, you have to go the extra mile. You have to make others like you and trust you. (And, yes, my famous hair style does grab one's attention, but I have to put in the work, as well.) After all, you are helping clients conduct one of the largest transactions in their lives. This significant event is literally in your hands. When I first began, I was scared every single day. I didn't know what I was doing, and my shyness kept me shackled in chains.

Ditch the Plan B

I agree to an extent there is some merit to establishing a Plan B in your life if your initial plan falls apart at the seams. I get it. You need a backup method of earning money and supporting yourself. I respect that. But a Plan B was less of a safety net for me and more of an excuse not to totally immerse myself in my entrepreneurial endeavors. If I was to support myself through a job that was strictly commission, I knew I had to be all in all the time. No buts. No excuses. No back up plan. I am an all or nothing kind of gal, and this was a terrific opportunity for me to showcase that philosophy.

I have always been the one who will go get what I set my mind to do. I have always known what I want my life to look like and also what I don't want it to look like. I keep that vision clear in my head. I cannot afford to fail, so I continually do whatever it takes to get that paycheck.

Network! Network! Network! (Then Repeat, Keeping this Habit on a Continuous Loop!)

When I first started out as a Realtor, no one at that time would have ever dreamed I would achieve success as I have. In the past, when I walked into a room, many might not have even noticed I was there. Today, I am a networking queen and proud of it! When I go to an event, by the end of that event, at least 90% of the people there will know me. I have honed my networking prowess over the last 10 years to a level 10. I am out there because I believe this business – and most any business, really – is a face-to-face business. Most of my clients will tell me they chose me initially because they might have seen my photo online and deemed it trustworthy, and then when they finally meet me, my personality and willingness to serve them seals the deal. I am not about the sale. No, I didn't stutter when I said that. It is not about the sale for me. What? Are you kidding me? Don't you want to close the transaction and earn some money? Of course, I do, but if I approach the situation with only the sale in mind and only the sale at top of mind, I will never close the deal. The relationship I build throughout each transaction is what leads to success. This client-based approach is what has allowed me to build my business mainly from referrals over the years. I would say that 90% of my business is solely based on others referring people to me because of their positive experience with me. Again, I do what is in the best interest of my clients. I solve problems. I make things happen. I do what it takes to get things done and I refuse to cut corners in the process. Some folks have jokingly referred to me as a "*pit bull in a skirt*." I'll take that compliment because I work hard and I make sure that my clients get not only what they want but also what is right for them. I won't hold back if I think a house is not right for them. My goal is to not only put money in my pocket at the end of the day, but also to put more money into my clients' pockets!

Some may raise a skeptical eyebrow, but if I have a client who has to bring money to the table, I will work with them on getting help from the bank and or discussing a commission reduction to help that person out. Why? Because if that client has a positive experience with me, then he or she will tell several other people. And, in all honesty, I don't have the time to look for clients. I have come to learn that if you do your job right and well, you will never have to look for clients ever. They will naturally seek you out based on what they hear from others. The more you give, the more you get. It's a very simple equation once you understand it. Say what you mean and mean what you say, always...and without fail.

Don't Be Afraid to Keep Current with Technology

Technology. It's an awesome thing. It has done wonders for so many aspects of business, especially in real estate. Don't be afraid to use it. If I never embraced technology, I would still be using the same Kodak camera I used in the initial stages of my career to take photos of homes! With a client list that includes buyers and sellers internationally, the advances in technology have been a game changer for me. When I have clients who are half-way around the world, it can be rather tricky when it comes to faxing disclosure agreements to someone in Qatar, for example, if not downright impossible. Even if I could send a fax to someone in another country, I could not be entirely certain it was received in its entirety or that it even reached my client. Then there is the anxiety that comes with sending confidential financial information overseas. For those things, I would often have to resort to costly, time-consuming overnight couriers, which could put the deal in jeopardy.

As someone who loves to learn and keep pace with what is going on in my industry, I knew there had to be a better way to get this accomplished. This is when DocuSign entered my world. While attending a National Association of REALTORS® technology course (always learning!) for my e-PRO® designation, a colleague was speaking about the advantages of eSignature technology. That got my attention. I was growing weary of tracking people down to get a signature and as I mentioned, faxing documents half-way around the world was a total nightmare at times. Fortunately, most everyone has a computer or smartphone. After doing my research, I chose DocuSign for its convenience, flexible pricing and security. From the first time I used it, I was hooked. Now a client in Egypt, for example, can receive and sign documents quickly and with peace of mind, knowing his or her sensitive information is not at risk. When you work in an industry where time is of the essence, as often multiple bids are being sent simultaneously on a property, eSignature is a highly competitive tool for my buyers to preempt other offers by being the first presented to the seller.

This tool has also increased my productivity, as I can quickly create documents and obtain eSignatures. Forms can be completed and sent within minutes, safely and securely. I no longer have to track clients down for signatures or missing initials on documents, which is great in a fast-paced market where being first in line can make all the difference in the world. This form of technology has allowed me to stay on top of my game, so my clients come out winners.

Full disclosure: In all honesty, I am not always highly organized, but I do know where everything is in the chaos. I have to admit that it took me until this year to use a CRM. I used to just keep all of that information in my head, but I understand a business needs structure. Thank goodness I have developed a strong association with technology. At the very least, it helps me to remember all of my clients, past and present, to whom I should deliver my annual Thanksgiving pies and

Christmas tree ornaments! Also, having a plan of your daily activities is essential to your success.

Remember! It's Only Money!

When people ask me if there is anything I'd change about myself, my honest answer is nothing. There is nothing I would change about myself at this time. I change as time requires me to change. When the market was down several years ago, I found myself frozen, mentally paralyzed and unable to make decisions. I lost money, and not just a little bit. I lost A LOT of it, in addition to stocks, my 401k and several properties. But I had to remind myself that "it's only money." Once I accepted that idea, I was able to pull myself together and realize who I really was. I am Nancy Alert. I get things done! I never allowed myself to sit and think about what I have lost, mainly because I have so much to gain.

"Fear causes hesitation, and hesitation will cause your worst fears to come true."

— Patrick Swayze as Bodhi in Point Break, 1991.

That quote certainly hit home. Any sign of hesitation or weakness on my part would only bring to light my worst fears. As such, I could not skip a beat, miss a turn, or neglect an opportunity. I had to keep moving forward. There's a reason why the rearview mirror is smaller than the windshield, and I had to learn to keep my eyes steadily focused on the road ahead.

So, in reality, I suppose I have a lot of powers that continually keep me on the path to success, but I suppose the one super power that works for me the most is that I am Nancy Alert. That is who I am. I am my personality. That is what people see. Your super power is also who you are.

Affirm who you are and what it is you desire to achieve.

Real estate is my career; it is my business. It is not just a job, and one I intend to always do well and correctly. I want people to come to me feeling that I am the best at what I do. I want to instill that sense of confidence in my clients. I can honestly say that I am the best at what I do. Why? Because I always, always, always keep my clients' best interests at heart. When I rest my head on my pillow at night, I have solid peace of mind knowing I did the right thing throughout the day. Am I perfect? No. But I never miss the mark when it comes to doing the right thing. I also summarize the overall day in my head – how it went and how I can improve upon that tomorrow.

I am also a sucker for affirmations. I keep several of them posted in my home and in my car. They are my mental vitamins. One of my favorite ones is as follows, which I keep posted on my closet door, so I see it the last thing before I go to bed at night and first thing upon awakening in the morning:

"The will to win, the desire to succeed, the urge to reach your full potential... these are the keys that will unlock the door to personal excellence."

— Confucius

I also have a vision board, which I periodically updated. Interestingly enough, when I first began using vision boards, I had a white Lexus on them, and to this day, all of my cars have been White Lexus brands.

I prefer to partner my affirmations with inspiration from others who have led before us, and this includes Napoleon Hill. A couple of his passages that speak loudly to me are as follows:

Faith is a state of mind, which may develop by conditioning your mind to receive Infinite Intelligence. Applied faith is the adaptation of the power received from Infinite Intelligence to a definite major purpose. Both poverty and riches are the offspring of thought. When faith is added to thought, the subconscious mind instantly picks up the vibration. Translates it into its spiritual equivalent and transmits it to Infinite Intelligence. Faith is the only agency through with the cosmic force of Infinite Intelligence can be harnessed and used. You can do it if you believe you can.

"Whatever the mind can conceive and believe, the mind can achieve."

Definiteness of Purpose is the starting point of all achievement. Don't be like a ship at sea without a rudder, powerless and directionless. Decide what you want, find out how to get it, and then take daily action toward achieving your goal. You will get exactly and only what you ask and work for. Make up your mind today what it is you want and then start today to go after it! Do it Now! Successful People move on their own initiative, but they know where they are going before they start.

What if you read these statements each time you made a phone call, or texted, or received a call? Imagine the possibilities of auto-suggesting this puts into your mind hundreds of times per day.

I have no shame in referring to myself as one-of-a-kind, both in and out of this industry. I say that not with ego or arrogance, but with utter confidence in what I can do for others. Whenever people meet me, I want them to walk away feeling they have met a unique and interesting person, one whose name alone resonates with something positive and exciting. (Yes, I admit...the hair does have a personality all of its own! Why do you think I keep it this way? It's definitely a hallmark of mine, and a great conversation starter!)

Parting thoughts...

Certainly, in most any given industry, especially if you choose to remain in it for the entirety of your career, it is a challenge to come out on the other side relatively unscratched. That being said, though, there are ways you can greatly minimize the discomfort of down times, and that is to adhere to one simply philosophy that always seems to keep me going:

Remember to remain one for whom kindness and compassion for others are genuine instincts; honesty is a lifestyle; and joy and passion for what you do are habits.

And if you are one of those people who, for efficiency's sake, merely skim a chapter and read the first paragraph and then race to the end, well I will save the best for last. This way, you won't miss out on the opportunity to understand, from my experience, the 10 "*Must-Dos*" for a successful sales career in real estate (but these are applicable in so many disciplines). I suggest you commit these not only to memory, but also to habit.

1. Be on time.
2. Be consistent.
3. Make prospecting a priority.
4. Understand and implement time management strategies.
5. Know your market or product.
6. Exercise effective and open communication skills.
7. Always, always follow-up.
8. Set the appropriate expectations.
9. Say what you mean and mean what you say.
10. Be Honest with your clients (I cannot overstate this one!).

Remember! You don't have to be a sales professional when it comes to real estate. If you excel at "*selling*," that's great, but it is not a pre-requisite. Work more on your relationship building skills. You are an educator, an advocate, a consultant, and a trusted advisor. And, if the relationships you build flourish and grow over the years, you will also become a friend to your clients.

Nancy Alert | Bio

Since 1996, Nancy Alert has led a successful real estate practice in the Washington, D.C. area, with licenses in Washington DC, Maryland and Virginia. Alert, a Howard University graduate with a Bachelor of Science in Marketing and another in Environmental Science and Design, coupled with a long list of designations, represents residential and commercial clients in buying, selling or leasing. Nancy routinely serves buyers and sellers internationally, especially from Egypt, Middle East, Mexico and Dubai.

Nancy was nominated into RE/MAX Hall of Fame for earning over a million dollars in two years; highlighted in Who's Who in Black Washington, DC; and featured as a technology innovator in Black Enterprise Magazine. Nancy served as the executive producer for the anti-bullying-event, Bully Free Beautiful Me, and has made several speaking appearances for various women's business organizations, local schools, and universities, including her alma mater's Communications Department's Advanced Public Relations class. She is a committed and socially conscious entrepreneur who lends her expertise and unconventional approach to businesses and women's organization in her role as a speaker and teacher. Nancy also served as the Editor-in-Chief for HerLife Magazine. She is a tech savvy, culturally diverse Realtor, an excellent communicator and negotiator whose business acumen lands her at the top of her game as a Real Estate Broker.

Because of the help she received early in her career, Nancy dedicates appreciable time to her community, serving as an example, a teacher, and a speaker with intention to build, inspire and empower other women. Giving back has always been in style for Nancy, and she hopes to make a positive difference for those around her every day as a result.

Company: Nancy Alert & Associates L.L.C. an affiliate with Better Homes & Gardens Real Estate

Location: Washington DC Metro Area

Website: www.nancyalert.com

Email: RealEstate@NancyAlert.com

CHAPTER 8

The Pursuit of Freedom!

By Brian Linh Nguyen

Have you ever experienced a really bad dream where you were being chased by a terrifying monster only to find you have been unable to elude it despite desperately trying really hard to run away as fast as possible?

My father, mother, and two younger brothers lived that dream in the summer of 1984 when we tried to escape from our country of ancestry in pursuit of freedom. The setting was in the small town of Ben Tre, located south of Ho Chi Minh City, Vietnam. Our goal was to head westbound in the hope of ending up in the United States of America. To achieve our goal, we first had to outrun the aforementioned terrifying monster known as the communist soldiers of Vietnam. The soldiers were armed and would not hesitate for a second to shoot and kill all of us in the event we got caught in order to prevent us from fleeing the country.

In preparation for our departure on one fateful summer night in 1984, my father went ahead to make sure the path to our small boat was clear. As we all waited patiently for my father to return, our other relatives who were also joining us on our escape to

America were growing more and more impatient. As a result, we all had to leave immediately to the boat where my father was located.

During this time, I was only six years old. My middle brother, David, was four and my youngest brother, Steven—who was still in my mother's arms—was only two years old. Running to the boat in the dark with three young boys was no easy task for my mom. We had to be hasty while being very quiet to prevent being discovered by the communist soldiers. By the time we arrived at the boat, my father was nowhere to be found because he had already headed back to the house to get us. We tried to wait for my dad to return but my relatives and other members of the group grew very impatient and insisted that we leave immediately. By the time my dad figured out that we had already left from the house and headed back to the boat, we were all gone. Aside from the devastation of being away from his family, my dad was also thrown in jail for the next six months as a result of his failed attempt to flee the country.

THE CHASE

Once we departed from the shores of Vietnam, we took a small boat to a larger vessel where we were greeted by the captain and crew of the ship with much anticipation. At that point, we were ready to begin our journey southward to Malaysia. We thought it would be smooth sailing from there, but this was far from the case. After we traveled for about half an hour, we began to hear the sounds of loud thundering and a pop noise from behind us. To our disbelief we were being chased down and followed by the communist soldiers at a distance. It appeared we were discovered. The loud crackling sound we heard were from the weapons on their ship firing at us. Luckily, no one was hurt from the shooting. More importantly, our ship did not incur any damages from all the shootings since they were too far for the bullets to reach us. We were pursued for nearly six long hours before the communist soldiers gave up and headed back. My brothers and I were too young to remember all of the details but that was the longest six-hour period of our lives according to my mom.

Aside from the scary encounter with the communist party chasing us down, we were quite fortunate because we did not encounter any pirates at sea. In contrast, there have been numerous stories of other refugees who emigrated from Vietnam who came across pirates. The results of those unwelcomed meetings were truly frightening. Generally speaking, the people who traveled across the sea to start a new life elsewhere usually carried a large amount of gold and other assets with them, and many of these individuals were victimized by these thieving pirates—who were motivated and fueled by pure greed. In addition to falling victim to the numerous thefts at the hands of these pirates, women and younger children were also raped and killed by these scoundrels. These pirates typically emanated from the surrounding Asian countries such as Thailand, Laos, Cambodia, and Vietnam to name a few. As if it was not bad enough to think about pirates at sea, my family was constantly worried about the possibility of getting lost in the vast sea as we journeyed south to Malaysia.

After just three days of travel at sea, we were beginning to run out of food and water. I vaguely remember at one point during our voyage when we had to cook rice with the seawater because we did not have any more fresh water left. It was difficult to eat, but we had no choice. On our fourth day, we had no water and very little to no food left. The thought of dying from starvation and dehydration was becoming a reality. At this point, we were beginning to doubt whether we were heading in the right direction. Just as we thought all hope was lost, we saw a beacon of light in the night. It was the brightest and most beautiful thing we had ever seen. It was an oilrig! We were very fortunate to get assistance from these generous people. They gave us food, water, and pointed us into the right direction. A day later, we finally made it safe and sound to Malaysia!

My family spent the next six months in a Malaysian camp before getting shipped to the Philippines. While waiting for all of our paperwork to be processed for approval, we had to spend another six months in the Philippines. During that time, my brothers and I went to school and learned some English. In 1985, we made it to America.

It was not until ten years later in 1995 that my dad was finally able to reunite with the family by sponsorship. By then, my brothers and I were all grown and were in our teens.

So why did my parents go through great lengths and danger to emigrate the whole family away from Vietnam? It was because Vietnam is a poor, communist nation with little or no opportunity for the average family to make something of themselves.

Unless one was an important official of the government or a successful business tycoon, it was hard to maintain a comfortable living in Vietnam. Unlike Vietnam, America is one of the greatest nations with ample opportunity for all as long as individuals are willing to work hard for it. Oftentimes, people in America forget what a great privilege it is to live in one of the richest nations in the world.

My parents took the risk to give my two younger brothers and I the opportunity to have more—opportunities they did not receive when they grew up in Vietnam. This was the biggest gamble they had made, but in the end, we were very lucky and it paid off. The risk was great but the reward was greater. Migrating to America was the best gift my parents ever gave us.

ASSIMILATION

My family started our new life in America. We arrived in San Jose, California in 1985. At the beginning, we stayed with our mom's cousin, Nancy La. We started going to school shortly thereafter. The first step of assimilation was to obtain new American names to be used in school in order to make it easier for others to refer to us since our names were difficult for some to pronounce. We initially liked the idea, but in retrospect, it was unnecessary. The names given to us were Brian, David, and Steven—some of the most commonly used American names. When combining our common American first names with our common Vietnamese last name, the ensuing result was Brian, David, and Steven Nguyen, which made differentiating my brothers and I from other individuals possessing the same names to be difficult. I wish we were given more unique names.

The next step of assimilation was to learn the culture and language. English is a strange and very complicated language for non-native speakers because its roots and structure are borrowed from other languages. The spelling of words are unpredictable, and minor changes in verbal pronunciation result in altering the meaning of a specific word. For the native speakers, speaking English is an easy task, but the opposite holds true for foreigners. Initially, much of this did not make sense, but because we were children, it was easier for my brothers and I to learn and pick up the language. Unfortunately, we cannot say the same for our mother. Our mom has a heavy accent, and most of the time her tongue and mouth feel very stiff when speaking and pronouncing English words. It was a culture shock for our mom, but she did not complain and did her best to raise her three sons on her own.

As a result of my mother's limited skills in English, she had to clean other people's homes and scrub toilets for low pay in order to support her three sons. We also had the good fortune of receiving government assistance. Even though we were poor, as American residents, we were given the opportunity to get free educations and assisted living. We would not have received government assistance of this kind if we continued to live in Vietnam.

Although we were poor, we always had each other. Maybe this was one of the reasons why my brothers and I are so close with strong bonds. As first-generation Vietnamese-Americans, we had to figure things out on our own. There was no one to guide or teach us. As the eldest of the three brothers, I guided my brothers through the process since I was always the one to experience everything first. I always tried to look after them and guide them as much as possible so that they did not make the same mistakes I did.

I am proud to say that my mom and dad are true Americans heroes. They risked everything to bring us to

America and put my brothers and me through college. David and I graduated from San Jose State University, while Steven graduated from UC Berkeley. My parent did quite well for themselves as they were able to live the American dream. Today we are all proud United States Citizens. They are also proud home owners.

SCHOOLING

When I first started school, I was scared out of my mind. I was in a new environment, culture, school system, and I did not speak a single word of English. What I was afraid of most was I could not speak or understand the language. I had no clue what I was going to do with myself. I was terrified because I was around strangers who spoke a foreign language I did not understand. Even at a young age, I was thinking to myself, "*how in the world am I going to get through this,*" and if I somehow emerged from the experience, what was I going to subsequently do to be a contributing member of society. The uncertainty was very overwhelming.

At school, I was very quiet and kept to myself. I was very shy back then. Although I would never initiate or start a conversation with others, I would talk to others if they spoke to me. At least I was not one of those painfully shy individuals. I was, and still am, an introvert.

I learned English by listening to my teachers, listening to others, and watching how people communicated on television; then, I slowly picked up the language.

In middle school, I felt I was not the smartest or brightest compared to some of the other kids, but I went through the motions anyway. However, what I did have was determination and grit. I simply tried a lot harder than most of the other kids in school. I went to all of my classes and was never late or missed a day of school even if I was sick because I did not want to fall behind. I tried doing as much of the homework as I could even if I knew my work may have been incorrect. I had no choice since there were no one else who could help, especially not my mom. Because of my determination and hard work, I was able to obtain straight A's throughout my years in school.

During my time in high school, I was introduced to the game of basketball and soon developed a love for the game. I was convinced by some friends to try out for the team. I tried out made the high school junior varsity and varsity basketball teams in my junior and senior years of high school respectively. Being actively involved in extracurricular activities enabled me to step outside of my introverted shell by meeting and mingling with others outside of the classroom. Because of my experiences on the junior varsity and varsity teams, I developed a love and a strong passion for the game of basketball.

During the course of middle school, high school, and college, I had roughly more than a dozen jobs as a young teenager. Most of my jobs were in the summer. This enabled me to have extra spending money and gave me a measure of independence, which in turn helped my mom focus her attention on my two younger brothers.

After high school, I was accepted and attended a local college nearby. By staying local, I was able to save money and live at home. After attending San Jose State University, I was able to secure a bachelor's degree in Business Management with a focus in Management Information System and a minor in Economics.

Throughout my years in high school, I did not get involved with extracurricular school activities beyond playing basketball. I did not attend any dances, promos, or any other activities outside of attending the required classes. After college, I told myself I could not live like that and needed to make a change. From that point forward, I told myself that I would take the initiative to be more personable. It was difficult at first but I took the initiative to open up to people. I approached people first, initiated conversations, and just made a point to be genuinely interested in the people whom I spoke with. Because I was stepping outside my comfort zone, I initially felt uncomfortable, but I forced myself to continue talking to people, and my comfort level grew as I spoke to more people. What I have learned from my experience is people are generally good once I make a point to get to know them.

THE FINANCIAL INDUSTRY

In 2002, I graduated from San Jose State University. By the time I graduated, the tech bubble had burst and I was unable to secure a job in the field I went to school for. I thought to myself, "*Did I waste the last five years of my life in college for nothing?*" What I came to realize was school was not only about learning your craft, but it also taught me how to be more disciplined, how to find answers, and how to solve problems as well.

Most people who graduate in their respective fields oftentimes do not work in the field they studied for. This is usually the case for most college graduates 73% of the time.

Next, I found myself working in the financial industry at Citibank. While working at Citibank, I learned that my position was not simply a paper-pushing job, but it was more of a sales job because I was required to sell many of the bank's products to current and new customers. I was a New Accounts and Loan Specialist. In order to sell and talk about some of the products, I was required to obtain an insurance and securities licenses (Series 6 and 63). As an introvert, I never, in my wildest dreams, imagined myself as a sales person.

After my time at Citibank, I became employed by a Credit Union where I was an Account, Loan and IRA Specialist.

ENTERPREURIAL SPIRIT

During my employment at the Credit Union, I, along with my partner, opened up a business. My partner, Thy Sok, and I concurrently worked full time at the Credit Union. We worked on our Internet Café business on the weekend and opened it up after the setup and renovations were complete. Once the business was up and running, we had a few workers to manage the place. It was great at first but eventually it failed because of its long distance. As they say, no one cares about your business more than you do. Because of the distance of the business's location, we were not able to look after it regularly and give it the constant attention it needed. The only time we were able to visit the business was on the weekends when we were off from our day jobs. Additionally, the cost to update the software and hardware was very expensive to upkeep and maintain. After two years of operation, we had to call it quits.

Although our business failed, I still have love and passion for businesses and the opportunities they bring.

HOUSING BUBBLE

The housing bubble lead up to the recession from 2007 to 2009. I too was caught in the game of home speculation. At the height of the bubble, I speculated in the housing market along with millions of other Americans and was badly burned. Like most, I was highly leveraged with some really bad ARM (adjustable rate mortgages). The lesson learned from living through the tech and housing bubbles was sometimes it is better to opt for investments that provide slower and safer returns rather than opting for the high risk/high reward associated with more leveraged investments. The great Warren Buffet once said, "*Be fearful when others are greedy and be greedy when others are fearful.*" These sage words rang true during the tech and housing bubbles, and they continue to be applicable today. As I have grown older and wiser, I have learned to take more calculated risks. I still have the entrepreneurial spirit in me and will not stop trying until I get it right.

GOING THE EXTRA MILE - REAL ESTATE BROKER

"The most successful people are those who serve the greatest number of people."

After leaving the Credit Union and exiting the financial industry, I obtained my real estate broker license and joined my brother along with a college buddy at Coldwell Banker. It was an easy transition as my brother was already at Coldwell Banker for more than ten years with a wealth of knowledge. He guided me and taught me everything I needed to know so that I could be successful. I was blessed to have him because generally, in the real estate space, people are very secretive about their trades. This is especially true in their marketing campaign.

In addition to my real estate license, I am also licensed as an insurance agent and public notary from my banking job. This was especially helpful for my clients since these were complementary services to real estate. Clients were particularly appreciative of my ability to assist them in more ways than one.

As a real estate sales professional, I learned my craft to the best of my ability in order to help as many people as possible in the most efficient manner. To implement this, I had to put a system in place to combine maximum effectiveness and efficiency. With a background in business and computer, I was able to automate most of the common processes. These included sharing a Dropbox with other team members, creating a master spreadsheet to track my progress, automate and schedule social media postings, and create templates for common forms used. I also created videos and website contents to address common questions and concerns people had in the buying and selling process. At the beginning, a lot of time and work was invested into putting a system in place, but upon doing so, life became easier. The system enabled me to help a lot more people in a shorter amount of time.

I learned that by being good at solving peoples' problems through addressing their most important needs and desires, I will be rewarded handsomely. As

Thomas Jefferson once stated, "*the harder I work the luckier I get,*" which is absolutely true.

As an introvert person, I never imagined that I would one day end up becoming a professional sales person. I am truly grateful and blessed to be a true sales professional.

PLEASING PERSONALITY

"It is essential that you develop a pleasing personality – pleasing to yourself and others."

As a professional in the sales industry, I pride myself in being the best at what I do and serving people to the best of my abilities.

During my selling career, I have had many mentors, but the mentor that resonated with me was Mark Fluker because I learned the most from him. In addition to being a cherished mentor, Mark is a very close personal friend. He once told me because I am an unassuming person with a pleasing personality, I will go far and do well for myself in my endeavors. He also reminded me not to change who I am and to be myself. He has forever etched this concept into my mind for as long as I live.

Mark Fluker is a straight shooter and will tell you how it is. He is a very strong individual both mentally and physically with strong work ethics. All in all, he is a really great guy and I am truly blessed to have him in my life as a personal friend and mentor.

Mark taught me the following three concepts, which I found to be very helpful and have assisted me in my selling career.

#1 NOT ALL MONEY IS GOOD MONEY

Sometimes you just have to recognize that not all money is good money and to cut your losses. Once you know the person you are working with is not worth the trouble, headache, and aggravation, it is better to cut your losses and move on. I learned that it is very important to define who my ideal clients are and to find ways to seek out those individuals to work with. It is better to deal with people who are like myself, easy to deal with, and just a pleasure to be around. The difficult clients I serve will usually take 80% of my time and only account for 20% of my sales. In contrast, the ideal clients I want to serve will usually take only 20% of my time but will account for 80% of my sales results. Whenever possible, apply the 80/20 rule for more positive results.

#2 PRICE IS WHAT YOU PAY, VALUE IS WHAT YOU GET

When I am selling a product, I need to build value in what I am selling in order for the price to be justified. I need to point out all the features, benefits, and enjoyment that a product will bring to my clients in order to justify the price they are paying for the product. For example, let's assume I am looking at two dress shirts. One shirt from Calvin Klein is priced at $100 and the other shirt from Gap is priced at $20. Why should I buy the Calvin Klein dress shirt over the Gap dress shirt when it is 5 times the price of the Gap shirt? This is where value needs be to be built. Maybe the Calvin Klein shirt is made from a higher-quality wrinkle-free material that will appear to look new no matter how many times it is washed. Because of these features and benefits, its price will be justified and now it will be worth the price the client will pay, but these features need to be communicated to the client by me, the salesperson, in order for the client to understand the value proposition.

#3 DON'T TURN A QUESTION INTO AN OBJECTION

Do not turn a question into an objection. Oftentimes, when a customer asks a question, they just want the question to be addressed. The trouble that some salespeople run into is rather than answering a client's question clearly and concisely, they dance around it, justify it, or sometimes avoid it completely. This oftentimes will bring up more questions and issues that were not present to begin with. Now, instead of addressing one issue, the salesperson will now have to juggle four other issues along with the original one. In some cases, when you do not know the answer, just let the client know that you do not have the answer but will find out and get back to him/her later before moving on. Makes sure to make a mental note of the question and address it later. A good rule of thumb to apply is the KISS rule; keep it simple and straightforward.

IN LOVING MEMORY OF TOM TOO TALL CUNNINGHAM

I would like to leave some thoughts and prayers for the "*Simply Amazing*" Tom Too Tall Cunningham and his family. During the writing of this book, Tom passed away suddenly while recovering from one of his many surgeries in his life. It was truly shocking and with great sadness. I wish we could have finished the book so that he could have had the opportunity to read our stories. I cannot describe how heartbreaking it is to see a friend go at the young age of 55 and cannot imagine what his wife, Kim, and family are going through. I hope that by writing this, I have made some impact in few people's lives and that I can make Tom proud. Thank you, Tom, for giving me the opportunity to share my story with the world. You will be missed. In loving memory of the most inspiring and positive person I know. May you rest in peace my friend!

Brian Linh Nguyen | Bio

Brian Linh Nguyen is a driven, charismatic, and passionate licensed real estate broker, insurance agent and public notary. He is committed to high professional standards, transparency, and honesty.

Brian was born in Me Tho Vietnam and is fluent in Vietnamese.

Brian graduated from San Jose State University. He obtained a Bachelor of Science degree in Business Administration with a concentration in Management Information Systems (M.I.S) and a minor in Economics.

Brian and his beautiful wife Han Nguyen, who is a Doctor of Pharmacy, currently reside in Las Vegas Nevada. Brian also loves kids and hope to have some of this own one day. Brian is the eldest of three brothers. His two younger brothers are David Nguyen and Steven Nguyen.

Brian has two dogs. A French bulldog named Piggy and a Chihuahua named Thi.

Brian loves anything that relates to business, real estate, and investing. In his spare time, Brian likes to play basketball and learn about the cryptocurrency revolution as a hobby. Brian also loves to share his knowledge and wisdom from his years' worth of experience.

When time permits, Brian and his wife love to travel the world and experience new cultures. They also love helping other people who are less fortunate.

To learn more about Brian, visit him at BrianLinh.com or contact him at Brian@BrianLinh.com

CHAPTER 9

Sell More, Help More

By Dave Doyle

Sales. Salesman. Saleswoman. Salesperson.

Is it just me, or do these words conjure up images of sleazy looking dudes in a used car lot, or someone going door-to-door with knick-knacks or gadgets?

I've been told for decades that I'm an amazing salesman and that I can sell anything to anyone, and the images above were, for a long time, the first things that I felt when I heard those words. When people told me how great a salesman I was, I would cringe. I thought to myself, "*wow, is that really what this person thinks of me? That I'm one of those salesman-y type of people?* "

I've always had a knack for persuasion, for providing a compelling argument for people to see my point of view, but I've never thought of it as salesmanship.

As I've grown through personal development and business development over the years, having built successful businesses in the franchise restaurant model and in direct sales, I've come to realize that '*sales*' is not a dirty word and salespeople are very rarely sleazy.

The fact is if you are a human being you are doing some sort of sales in the truest sense of the word every single day of your life.

We are always selling ourselves.

When we are dating, we are painting the best possible picture of ourselves in hopes of a second date.

Every day of our lives we either provide a product or service to a customer or client in our job or career, or we are the client/customer and often are selling ourselves to get the best deal.

How we interact with our kids, especially our toddlers and teenagers, is all sales. Just as often they are trying to sell to us with tactics like tantrums, guilt trips, compliments, favors, tricks, promises etc.

When we apply the perfect make up or put on that fitted shirt and tie, we are selling ourselves to someone somewhere to give the best impression that we can.

These examples are pure sales. Some people have more experience than others or maybe paint a prettier picture than others, but in essence it is all the same. I have heard so many people use this line over the years, "*yeah that sounds pretty interesting, but I'm just not a sales person, I don't know how to sell anything…*" and I don't buy any of it. Anybody can sell, but when it comes to doing it on purpose for pay we have to get into the right mindset.

I believe that when it comes to sales as a profession, there are two types of people:

The Professional Salesperson

First is the salesperson who can sell anything, anywhere and is completely comfortable and happy doing so. They are the serial sales professional who goes to the workshops, reads the books, sits in the sales seminars, studies the psychology of selling and how to close. You'll find many in traditional sales roles such as selling vehicles in dealerships, insurance, real estate, consultants and travelling sales reps for brands.

These are the types of individuals that most of the stereotypes have been built upon and though it may seem clear as to why, I contend that overall it is an unfair judgment.

In today's age my guess is that there are less of these types of sales professionals than the second type I'm about to describe, but some of the characteristics that stand out with these people is their courage, their discipline, their positive mental attitude in the face of rejection, and their dedication to their craft.

The Accidental Salesperson

The second type of sales person is the one that goes into business not realizing that their business is sales. I am one those people.

Before I opened my own restaurant, I managed three separate locations within the same franchise with the idea that I would own a location of my own in the future. My job was not simply to manage the team of employees and manage the day-to-day operation, but I was expected to increase sales by doing marketing to my customers within the restaurant and to potential customers outside the restaurant.

Did I feel like a *'salesman'* doing this kind of marketing?

Absolutely not. My belief system was that I was providing an amazing, healthy meal to anyone who visited. I was motivated to increase sales and do a great job for my employer to show that I can do this business and be worthy of owning my own location. I was also motivated to do this because I knew I would have to do the same things when I owned my own location, and this would prepare me. In my mind this was all just a part of business. I never considered myself a salesman doing sales calls, I was just *'promoting'*.

Promotions.

Marketing.

That's not selling, is it?

Of course it is.

The marketing team at that franchise later taught me that I wasn't a sandwich shop owner, I was a '*Marketing Agency*' that sometimes sold sandwiches. I didn't understand this at first but it finally did become clear. There are many aspects to owning and running a business, but if you can't get a handle on the Sales and Marketing aspects, it doesn't matter how good your operations and bookkeeping are, your business will be slow to grow. I learned to appreciate the sales aspect and be ok with being a salesman, I just didn't feel like the version of salesperson that I had always stereotyped in my mind. And that was great, because most salespeople are not that stereotype anyway!

When I started a home-based business in the direct sales industry about 10 years ago, it wasn't planned at all and I didn't consciously think to myself, "I'm now a salesman in this industry", but that's exactly what I became. It started with a product. A friend shared it with me (sold it to me) and I absolutely fell in love with it. A week later I was asking that friend how to get paid. It wasn't because I wanted a sales job, it was because I had a passion for the product and knew that if it worked for me, it would work for others and I was happy to share it.

This is why I call it an 'Accidental Salesperson'. It wasn't a job I applied for. I was not hired by someone to sell a product for a commission. I was recruited into a sales team to sell a product that I loved for a commission. What is the difference you may ask? Almost nothing.

I didn't plan on it, but I did it very quickly and easily.

And I became very good at it.

The Sales professional might apply at a corporation to sell their product or service because they feel they can bring value to the organization and make a significant income.

The accidental salesperson usually has an attachment or passion for the product or service first which leads to seeing an opportunity to share (sell) it with others and be compensated for that.

The professional salesperson leads with professionalism while the accidental salesperson leads with passion. Both paths lead to the same result; with the salesperdon being the provider of a product or service to someone who wants or needs that product or service. It is a noble profession that most people engage in at one time or another.

How Napoleon Hill has made me a better Salesperson

Jim Rohn said that we should work on ourselves more than we work on our jobs or our businesses. As I've developed my mindset, my character, my skills and my self-awareness through constant learning and personal development, I've simply become a better person; a better version of myself.

Through this process, it stands to reason that I've become better in many or all aspects of my life. Going deeper into the 17 Principles of success and learning to get better at living them every day has been the biggest influence in making me a great salesperson.

The reason that these 17 principles have stood the test of time and have been collectively, the single greatest influence of success for so many of the world's greatest success stories is that they are just that: Principles. They are not '*opinions*' of success. They are Principles, or Laws of success and when you set yourself upon the task of understanding them and living by them, you evolve faster into the person that you want to become; the person that you see yourself growing into.

It wasn't long ago that I felt that the word 'sales' and so much of what I thought that word meant, was tainted. Yet here I am, in the spring of 2018, writing a chapter for a book dedicated to success in sales. And to take it a step further, while I am writing these words I am in the process of partnering with a new company to lead a sales team in a brand new industry.

In the last 2 weeks alone, I have directly incorporated the Principles of Purpose, Mastermind, Applied Faith, Going the Extra Mile, Pleasing Personality,

Personal Initiative, Positive Mental Attitude, Enthusiasm, Self-Discipline, Accurate Thinking, Controlled Attention, Teamwork, Adversity & Defeat and Creative Vision towards the goal of building this Sales Team.

TOP 4 Tips for Evaluating a Sales Position

There are 4 criteria that I believe you should look for when evaluating an opportunity in sales.

First, believe in what you are doing. Either believe in the product you're selling or believe in the cause behind it. When you have a conviction that you are benefitting others through the product or service they are buying or by the service you are rendering, you will sell more and help more.

Second, believe in who you are working for. The Values, Mission and Vision of the company should always be in alignment with your own. If you feel good about who you are working for you will sell more and help more.

Third, believe in the Team around you and work alongside others that you can align with. Sales should never be a career where you feel alone. Find a supportive environment where even though there will always be competition, it should always be healthy and motivating. Find people who are positive and inspiring, people who help each other with accountability and drive everyone to be better which makes the company better and drives bonuses and perks. Individually you may be selling solo, but if you can work within a Team environment, you will sell more and help more.

Fourth, believe in yourself. You are the creator of your life. Follow Jim Rohn's advice and work on yourself daily. Learn something every day that makes you better in your work but learn things every day that aren't specifically work related as well. Evolve as a person and your sales will show it.

Believe, believe, believe and believe.

Sell more, help more.

We are all buying and selling every single day of our lives.

If you are in sales as a profession, congratulations! You are in an industry that is loaded with unlimited financial opportunity, personal growth and service to others. Thank you for all that you do.

Dave Doyle | Bio

Dave Doyle grew up training to be an entrepreneur.

He owns and operates two top performing restaurants in the Pita Pit franchise and he served for 4 years on Pita Pit Canada's Marketing Advisory Committee.

He has been a top performer since 2009 in his current business as an Independent Consultant with ORGANO International.

He was a founding member for three and a half years at the first BNI Chapter in his city and served as President in its second year.

Dave has been a student of personal development for almost 20 years. Since studying the 17 Success Principles of Napoleon Hill and taking the Leadership Certification Course through the Napoleon

Hill Foundation, he is driven to increase PMA around the world and has been a contributing Author to two other Amazon International Bestselling Books written by Napoleon Hill Students and Instructors.

He is now sought after as a speaker and trainer for individuals and corporations and is a co-creator of the Life Mastery Symposium.

Dave's passions are Business and Personal Development for himself and others but his 'Why' is his family. His wife Amanda and his two sons Ashton and Rhys fuel his passions and bring him home every day.

Please send a virtual Hi-5 to Dave at:

Email: pmaprofessor@gmail.com

LinkedIn: https://ca.linkedin.com/pub/dave-doyle/12/646/987

FB: https://www.facebook.com/pmadave/

Twitter: https://twitter.com/DaveDoylePMAPro

Instagram – davedoylemrpma

Napoleon Hill Bio

NAPOLEON HILL
(1883-1970)

"Whatever your mind can conceive and believe it can achieve."

—Napoleon Hill

American born Napoleon Hill is considered to have influenced more people into success than any other person in history. He has been perhaps the most influential man in the area of personal success technique development, primarily through his classic book Think and Grow Rich which has helped million of the people and has been important in the life of many successful people such as W. Clement Stone and Og Mandino.

Napoleon Hill was born into poverty in 1883 in a one-room cabin on the Pound River in Wise County, Virginia. At the age of 10 his mother died, and two years later his father remarried. He became a very rebellious boy, but grew up to be an incredible man. He began his writing career at age 13 as a "mountain reporter" for small town newspapers and went on to become America's most beloved motivational author. Fighting against all class of great disadvantages and pressures, he dedicated more than 25 years of his life to define the reasons by which so many people fail to achieve true financial success and happiness in their life.

During this time he achieved great success as an attorney and journalist. His early career as a reporter helped finance his way through law school. He was given an assignment to write a series of success stories of famous men, and his big break came when he was asked to interview steel-magnate Andrew Carnegie. Mr. Carnegie commissioned Hill to interview over 500 millionaires to find a success formula that could be used by the average person. These included Thomas Edison, Alexander Graham Bell, Henry Ford, Elmer Gates, Charles M. Schwab, Theodore Roosevelt, William Wrigley Jr, John Wanamaker, William Jennings Bryan, George Eastman, Woodrow Wilson, William H. Taft, John D. Rockefeller, F. W. Woolworth, Jennings Randolph, among others.

He became an advisor to Andrew Carnegie, and with Carnegie's help he formulated a philosophy of success, drawing on the thoughts and experience of a multitude of rags-to-riches tycoons. It took Hill over 20 years to produce his book, a classic in the Personal Development field called Think and Grow Rich. This book has sold over 7 million copies and has helped thousands achieve success. The secret to success is very simple but you'll have to read the book to find out what it is!

Napoleon Hill passed away in November 1970 after a long and successful career writing, teaching, and lecturing about the principles of success. His work stands as a monument to individual achievement and is the cornerstone of modern motivation. His book, Think and Grow Rich, is the all-time best seller in the field.

The Seventeen Principles

1. **Definiteness of Purpose**
2. **Mastermind Alliance**
3. **Applied Faith**
4. **Going the Extra Mile**
5. **Pleasing Personality**
6. **Personal Initiative**
7. **Positive Mental Attitude**
8. **Enthusiasm**
9. **Self-Discipline**
10. **Accurate Thinking**
11. **Controlled Attention**
12. **Teamwork**
13. **Learning from Adversity & Defeat**
14. **Creative Vision**
15. **Maintenance of Sound Health**
16. **Budgeting Time and Money**
17. **Cosmic Habitforce**

About John Westley Clayton

"You are who and what you create yourself to be"
—John Westley Clayton

Rock Star Maker, Bestselling Author, Publisher of Bestselling Books, Sales Trainer, Life Trainer, Life Mentor, Keynote Speaker... ROCK STAR!!!

John Westley Clayton is the publishing arm of the *Journeys To Success* series; and along with other multiple tiles to the John Westley Publishing brand, has come to represent quality within the industry.

Surviving a rough childhood, along with multiple setbacks, unbeknownst to John Westley, this fueled the fire for him to set out on his own and develop a pathway to success that fits his puritan work ethic. Through the years John Westley created a successful resume, outperforming in all areas of business, sales and management.

Through the years something started to awaken in him; only focusing on wealth development for years may have created physical comfort and freedom, but there was something missing. The pieces finally fell into place when he discovered *Think & Grow Rich* by Napoleon Hill.

Focusing on the prize of financial achievement alone wasn't enough; developing ones self as a well-rounded human being was the elusive secret John Westley had been looking for for years.

John Westley began manifesting a new reality and became a Napoleon Hill Certified Instructor, helping others achieve their goals.

As the CEO & Founder of John Westley Enterprises, John Westley has become the '*Rock Star Maker*' and the secret weapon behind many of today's thought leaders. Under his ***Rock Star*** *4 life* brand, he helps individuals build the life they want by stepping out of their comfort zone and onto a bigger stage. Providing group coaching, one-on-one mentoring, image and personal brand creation and publishing. John Westley's work brings Fortune 500 business solutions to a group of handpicked students.

For the past 10 years, he's been teaching entrepreneurs, educators, corporate leaders and people from all walks of life how to create the life they truly desire by making the choices that best serve them in their professional and personal lives.

Today, as a peak performance coach and personal development strategist, John Westley's programs have launched dozens of individuals into ROCK STAR status.

Got a dream? He'll place it center stage.

www.johnwestley.com

info@johnwestley.com

About Brad Szollose

Brad Szollose

(pronounced zol-us)

> *"...No one knows Millennials or cross-generational management better than Brad, and it shows; our attendees are still talking about his work."*
>
> — Robbins Research International, Inc., a Tony Robbins Company

TEDx Speaker, award-winning business author and Web Pioneer Brad Szollose helps businesses and organizations dominate their industry by tapping into the treasure of a cross-generational workforce. Brad has been called The Millennial Whisperer, and his Liquid Leadership workshops show attendees how to ignite the power of their workforce and their customer base.

Brad is also a global business adviser and the foremost expert on Generational Issues and Workforce Engagement. His bestselling book, *Liquid Leadership: From Woodstock to Wikipedia*, shares Brad's journey beginning as a bootstrapped business idea in a coffee shop to C-level executive of a publicly traded company worth $26 million in just 24 short months; becoming the FIRST Internet Agency to go public in an IPO!

As a C-Suite Executive Brad applied his unique management style to a young, tech-savvy Generation X & Y Workforce producing great results; The company experienced 425% hyper-growth for 5 straight years with only 6% turnover. Brad's management model won K2 the Arthur Andersen NY Enterprise Award for Best Practices in Fostering Innovation Among Employees.

Today the world's leading business publications seek out Brad's insights on Millennials, and he has been featured in Forbes, The Huffington Post, New York Magazine, Inc., Advertising Age, The International Business Times, The Hindu Business Line and Le Journal du Dimanche to name a few, along with television, radio and podcast appearances on CBS and other media outlets.

Today Brad's programs have transformed a new generation of business leaders, helping them maximize their corporate culture, expectations, productivity, and sales growth in The Information Age.

www.ingramcontent.com/pod-product-compliance
Lightning Source LLC
LaVergne TN
LVHW041317080426
835513LV00008B/502

* 9 7 8 1 9 4 7 5 6 0 0 4 8 *